ANATOMY OF THE
JOHN DEERE

Doug Mitchel

©2007 Doug Mitchel

Published by

krause publications
An Imprint of F+W Publications

700 East State Street • Iola, WI 54990-0001
715-445-2214 • 888-457-2873
www.krausebooks.com

Our toll-free number to place an order or obtain
a free catalog is (800) 258-0929.

Library of Congress Control Number: 2007923823

ISBN-13: 978-0-89689-553-9
ISBN-10: 0-89689-553-X

Designed by Thomas Nelsen
Edited by Tom Collins

Printed in China

Dedication

To my Dad.

He spent most of his life in the city, but found paradise in the country.

Acknowledgments

Being a newcomer to the field of John Deere tractors, I am deeply appreciative of those collectors who volunteered their time, and the tractors that you see pictured herein, to the success of this book. They not only rolled out their beautifully-restored machines for your viewing pleasure, they also dug into their resources to provide me with a vast quantity of research materials and information needed to create this book.

To my friend Jim Schneiter for allowing us to showcase a small portion of his collection of die-cast John Deere toy tractors.

Contents

1928 Model D

Until 1931, the John Deere Model D had the steering wheel on the left side.

John Deere entered the tractor business in 1918, when a decision was made to buy the Waterloo Gasoline Engine Company. The founders of Deere were already producing ancillary equipment for the tractor industry, but had yet to create a tractor that would bear the company's name. The Waterloo Boy was a unit already being built. It would remain on the order sheets until 1924. In the years between 1918-1923, the Model D was one of the prototypes developed. This fact would carry it into the Deere history books.

Introduced for the 1924 model year, the Model D embodied many of the legendary features that had grown in popularity on tractors from Ford, International Harvester and Allis Chalmers. Perhaps the most obvious of these was the lack of a frame. Instead of having the engine and its related hardware hang from an iron chassis, the Model D incorporated the engine and drive train castings as the frame of the unit. This arrangement created a stout assembly that would serve the farming community and John Deere well for three decades.

A two-cylinder engine that displaced 501 cubic inches powered the Model D. A smaller gasoline engine was used to get the primary engine running, from which point it ran on its own tank of kerosene. The year 1928 saw the D engine's bore size increased to 6.75 inches, which added a bit more power to the popular tractor and helped it sell well. The horizontal-twin engine was bolted to a two-speed gearbox, with another gear for reverse. Top speed for the D was a wild 3.25 mph. However, this solid tractor could maintain that speed for hours on end with no need to be fed or watered. The Standard Tread D, which was originally sold in only one configuration, would fill the needs of many a farm operator in the infancy of motorized harvesting.

With the D, another place where steel carried the load was in the wheels. All four corners of the tractor were fitted with steel wheels measuring 28 x 5 inches at the front and 46 x 12 inches at the rear. The current owner of this tractor added rubber strips to all four steel rims to permit use in local parades and other travel on paved roads. No adjustment for tread width was offered on these early Deere models. Late in the production of the 1928 models, a steel floor replaced the wooden slats of the early units. Enormous metal fenders wrapped around the rear wheels and provided a safe haven for the operator as his tractor tore through the fields.

The Model D performed well for John Deere, at least until the Great Depression took hold in 1929. This world-changing event took its toll on every facet of manufacturing and tractor sales were as affected, too. Surviving this dark economic period, Deere continued to improve the Model D. Sales of this venerable class leader would last until 1952, when a decision to retire the Model D was made. With 30 years of production in the "win" column, the Model D had been a terrific way for the John Deere Company to make its way into the crowded field of tractor manufacturing.

Whether you looked at the Model D from the front or the side, you knew it was a John Deere product.

▲ Fully-encompassing fenders were employed to protect the operator from errant clods of dirt and other stray detritus.

◄ Unlike later units that provided a plastic rim for the operator's hands, the 1928 John Deere Model D had only a steel wheel to steer the two-ton machine.

Above: *The lack of stylish sheet metal left basic parts like the radiator exposed for all the world to see.*

Top Right: *Early copies of the John Deere Model D wore open-spoke flywheels, while later editions carried these solid steel units.*

Right: *The owner of this D chose to add a rubber strap to the front wheels so that the tractor can be driven on paved streets during local parades.*

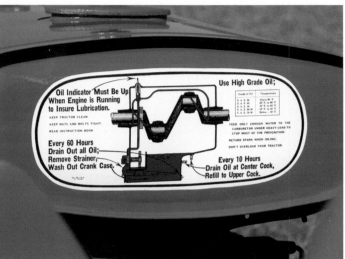

Far Left: The company logo with the leaping deer was prominently displayed on the John Deere Model D.

Left: This warning panel was affixed directly in the farmer's line of sight during tractor operation. It provided a constant reminder to keep his Model D properly lubricated.

The stubbiness of the 1928 John Deer Model D stands out as an overriding design trait.

To better compete with other tractors being sold, Deere released the GP to remain dominant.

n the mid-'20s, John Deere faced growing competition from International Harvester and knew that something needed to be done to regain market dominance. Deere perceived a need for a small, all-purpose tractor and began planning a new model to sell alongside its already-popular Model D. Prototypes for the new GP Standard were built in 1926 and development work continued into 1928. First named the Model C, Deere later chose the GP designation for this tractor to avoid confusion with the Model D.

After reviewing the machines being sold as Farmalls, Deere designer Theo Brown decided to include an arched front axle that splayed the wheels apart. This varied from the narrow design other manufacturers used. Due to the spacing and height of the design, Brown thought that the widely-spaced wheels could clear a third row of crops.

Deere's need to create a dominant model resulted in a number of other innovations being included in the C/GP model. The two-cylinder engine was of a new design fitted with side valves in place of the usual valve-in-head configuration. This was the first John Deere to feature an L-head engine and it displaced 311.6 cubic inches. Gasoline was used to start the C/GP, but it ran on kerosene once things were in motion. A 16-gallon tank held the operating fuel, while a two-gallon gasoline tank was used. Three forward and one reverse gear were found inside the gearbox. To simplify planting operations, the GP also featured a revolutionary new implement lift that was powered by the tractor. This meant the operator no longer had to stop, at the end of each row being planted, to manually lift the cultivator before turning. A foot pedal activated the lift and allowed the turning brake to pivot the GP into position. Once turned, the implement was lowered back into position for another row of seeding.

The new features of the GP were well received, but its performance in the field was not up to Deere's expectations. Due to its location, the air cleaner on early editions was prone to clogging, causing a lack of power. To prevent the air cleaner from pulling too much filth into the engine, in 1929 a taller stack was employed. The air cleaner was no longer in the direct path of flying soil and dust. Therefore, it delivered cleaner air to the engine, giving it more power and a longer service life.

The GP measured 112 inches in length and weighed 4500 pounds when loaded for operation. A rating of 24.97 belt horsepower was realized by the 1929 version. That number increased to 25.36 in 1931. The retail price for the 1927-1930 models was $800, without the addition of accessories and options.

The example of the John Deere GP pictured here wears several of the period accessories that were available directly through local John Deere dealers. Front and rear lighting was a welcome addition and was powered by a belt-driven generator that was coupled to the fan shaft. Protecting the radiator from flying debris was the Model AC-236 Radiator Guard. This one-piece device mounted in front

Although fairly compact the GP was designed to handle a variety of tasks.

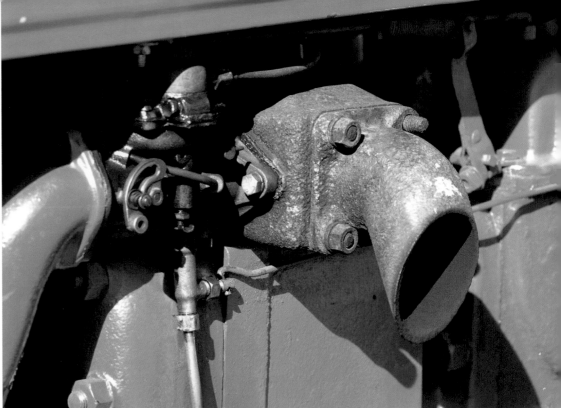

▲ The rotating exhaust elbow allowed the tractor user to deflect the exiting fumes in any desired direction.

◄ When starting the two-cylinder engine, excess fuel atomizes from the petcock. This alerts the operator that the fuel is reaching the engine as required.

Right: .On the 1929 GP, almost 25 belt horsepower was provided by the spinning clutch.

Far Right: In addition to being used as a starting mechanism, the cast flywheel keeps the engine running once it gets into motion.

By adding several factory options the uses of the GP were expanded.

Above Left: Mounted high on the radiator cap, this front light helped the farmer work into the dark hours of the night and added to his productivity.

Above Right: A steel steering wheel replaced the earlier wooden version. The steel wheel did a better job of withstanding the rough weather conditions encountered during long-time use of this tractor for field work.

Left: The accessory radiator guard and adjustable curtain on this 1929 GP protected the cooling fins and kept the engine running at the proper temperature.

of the radiator to prevent damage to the cooling fins and to keep passages from clogging. In order to keep the engine operating at the proper temperature under any conditions, an AC-435 Radiator Curtain was also added to this GP. The curtain could be raised or lowered to monitor the amount of air that reached the radiator, thus maintaining a proper temperature range whenever the tractor was in use. An AD-241 Exhaust Elbow has also been added to this tractor to help guide spent gases away from the engine. This device allowed the operator to deflect the flow of exhaust, in any direction, for his comfort.

The Model C/GP was produced through 1935. Once a few minor flaws had been corrected, this tractor was well received by tractor buyers. Just over 30,000 copies were sold from 1928-1935. The C/GP paved the way for introduction of the Model A.

1930 Model GP

As usual, the "John Deere" name was spelled out on block letters on the radiator tank and the sides of the hood.

Having previously discussed the John Deere GP model, it seems more important to discuss the long history of this Wide-Tread example in greater detail. Some vintage tractors have an easy life that leads to their eventual restoration, while others do not. This 1930 John Deere falls into the latter category. It has traveled a long way since being built in Moline, Illinois.

More than a decade ago, the tractor's current owner and his son were attending a show in Arkansas when a friend told them that a gentleman at the event had a GP for sale. The seller showed them pictures of the tractor, which was deeply embedded in a quagmire. The current owner eagerly agreed to buy the tractor, even though the seller wanted it clearly understood that the "rotting beast" was in poor condition and not in the best location. Neither of these concerns mattered to the buyer and a deal was struck.

A few months later, the new buyer and his son journeyed to Louisiana to recover the wretched tractor and bring it home. The old John Deere had been sinking into the same pool of mud for over 40 years, so the task at hand was not easy. However, the buyer remained undaunted by the challenge. He pulled the tractor free and the process of bringing it back to life began.

The tale of how the tractor ended up in a pool of mud was interesting. After purchasing the tractor new in 1930, the original owner placed the GP on a river barge to send it home. It would see use as a farmer's tool for 25 years. When a large flood was predicted, the farmer strapped a series of logs together to create a barge. Then, the tractor and some livestock were loaded onto the floating lift raft and kept there until the flood waters receded. When dry conditions returned, the GP was once again put into use. It kept working until 1955.

When one of the drive chains snapped inside the tractor's axle, the farmer simply got off the tractor, walked away and left it. The John Deere remained in that same spot for 40 years. Then, Sims McKnight and his son "rescued" it.

After retiring, Sims turned his attention to the restoration of the GP. He disassembled it down to its last nut and bolt. Inside, he found several tragic problems caused by the lengthy period of neglect and dampness. A gaping hole had rusted through the gearbox case and caused damage inside. Every tooth on the bottom of the transmission gears was rusted completely away and had to be replaced with teeth borrowed from a donor GP of the same vintage. The steel spokes of the "skeleton" wheels were in the same condition and portions of each of the lower spokes had to be fashioned from scratch and welded into place. Taking the place of the original skeleton cleats were new copies cast for the project. Along with the steel skeleton wheels on the rear axle, this example rolls on all steel "Texas" wheels up front. These were cast to achieve their unique contour.

It required nearly four years to complete the tractor's transformation, but the 1930 GP was fired up in 1998 using a 1935 John Deere Model A's drive belt to deliver the needed punch.

The last of the John Deere GP models was completed in October of 1933. It carried serial no. 405254 and was shipped to Uruguay.

From 1930 to 1935, the John Deere GP used an engine with a six-inch bore and stroke that had a governed speed of 950 rpm.

▲ This John Deere L-Head engine was exclusive to the C/GP.

◄ Mounted high to avoid some of the flying debris related to farming, this breather can draw fresh air into the engine.

1930 Model GP

Right: A storage box makes a handy place to carry small items that might be required out in the fields.

Far Right: The three forward gears and a single reverse gear could be engaged by depressing the clutch and using this sturdy gear-selection lever.

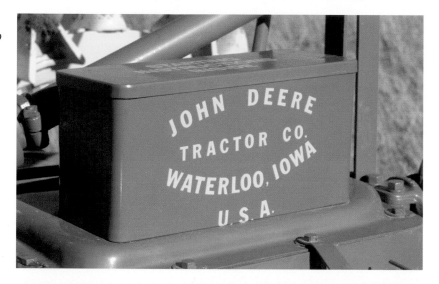

Projecting out behind the tractor, the farmer's perch on the 1930 John Deere GP was a real "cat-bird" seat.

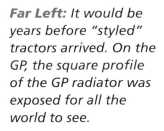

Far Left: It would be years before "styled" tractors arrived. On the GP, the square profile of the GP radiator was exposed for all the world to see.

Top Right: The flat steel used to create the rear wheels of early tractors gave them the nickname "skeleton wheels." The cleats were bolted onto the rim for easy replacement when necessary..

Bottom Right: Seen here in operation, the large cast flywheel keeps the engine in motion and also serves as a starting wheel.

The design of the 1935 John Deere Model A has numerous vertical elements like the tall radiator, the steering post and the twin breathers.

Being tractor collectors with some sense of restraint, the Germany family decided to narrow their growing collection of John Deere tractors to the so-called "letter" models. With a styled 1945 Model A already a part of his holdings, Randy Germany decided that an earlier "unstyled" Model A would make for a nice mix. His search led him to the 1935 edition you see here.

This tractor had rested in an open field for more than 15 years before it was discovered. It was buried halfway to the cases. A fire ant mound had also made the tractor home, so it took some doing to get it into the pristine condition we now get to see it in. The whole Germany family played a role in the Model A's restoration. Now, this tractor is a favorite at local parades and events.

Work on the new Model A began in 1931, while the country was still in the grips of the Great Depression. John Deere was aiming at a market that would survive even after the financial crisis of the early '30s had passed.

Several engineering factors were taken into consideration before the first sketches were done. The Model A engine was to be smaller, yet more powerful. It would go into a tractor that weighed less than its predecessor. The addition of a fourth speed to the gearbox was also another desired advancement. It would increase the tractor's usefulness around the farm.

Prototypes for the Model A were dubbed the FX. Work began using a 30-hp engine, but engineers found a 24-hp unit more desirable. As a result, rather than develop a new engine, it was decided that an existing two-cylinder design could be employed.

After two years of research and development, John Deere put together 10 more versions of Model AA experimental tractors. Then, in 1934, the first test models took to farm fields for real-world trials. Once these examples had proved their mettle, the first production-type Model A was delivered to a customer in March 1934.

The new design carried some innovations into the field, including an optional hydraulic lift for implement use. Some minor adjustments were made to production models, when certain conditions became apparent. The fuel cap was moved to the left of its original position to allow for better clearance from the steering shaft. Choices in the front axle column also grew as single-front-wheel and wide-front options joined the list.

The Model A was powered by a 309-cid engine that was fed by the all-gas method. Ratings of 975 rpm at the PTO and 24.71 hp at the belt were achieved on the first editions of the Model A. For fuel, a 14.5-gallon primary tank was fitted, with one-gallon held separately for the starting motor. Overall length of the 3,525-pound A was 124 inches. It sold for $1,050 through 1940.

Many configurations of the Model A were available. This 1935 edition is built in Row Crop configuration with dual tricycle wheels up front and an adjustable-width axle in the rear. Measuring from

1935 Model A

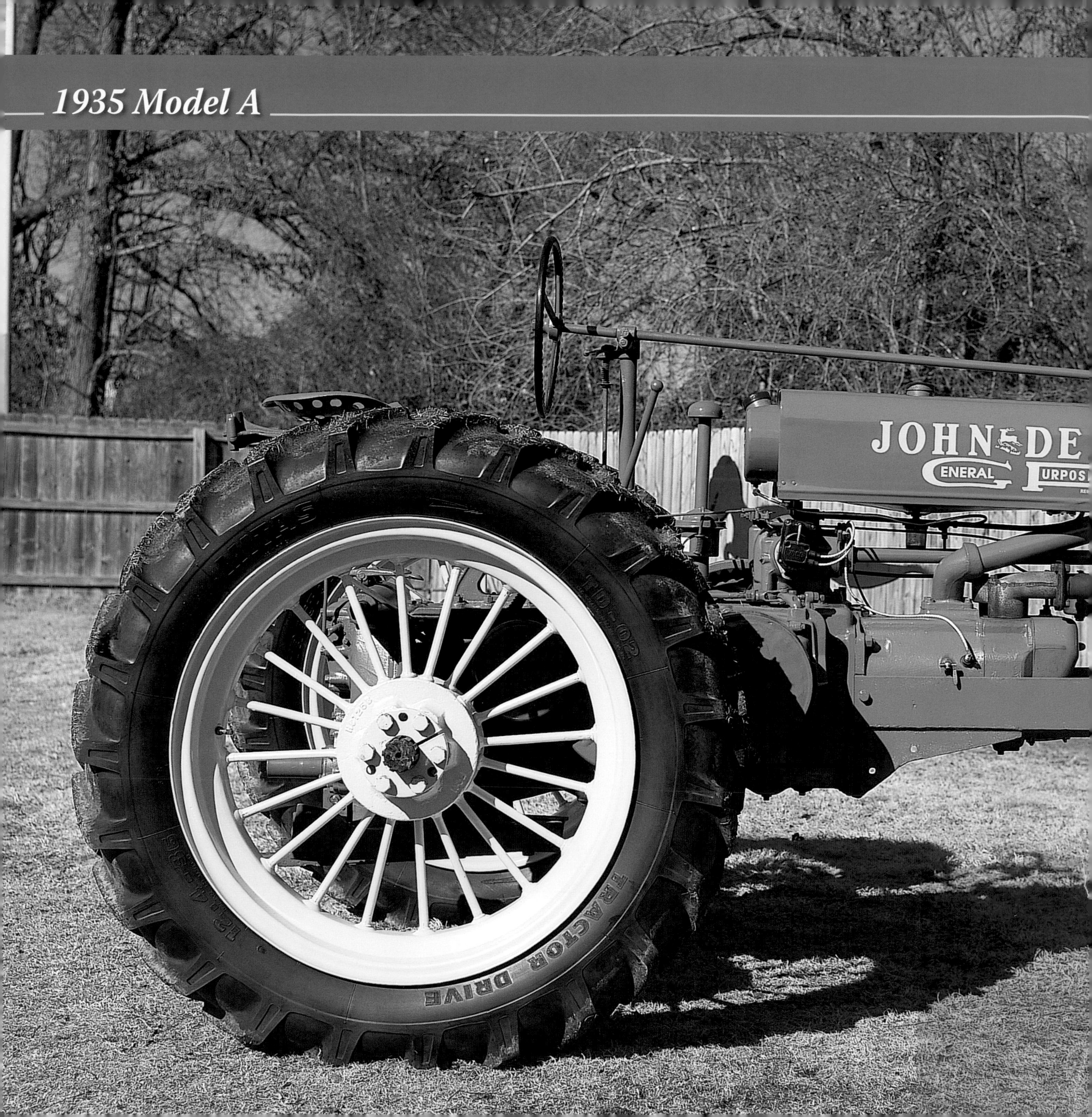

When viewed in profile the over-the-hood steering mechanism shows its length.

▲ *Early copies of the A and B held their steering pedestals in place with this four-bolt clamp. Later editions would switch to an 8-bolt clamp designed to better endure heavy use.*

◄ *Lacking the accoutrements of the styled units that arrived later, the 1935 John Deere Model A carried over-the-hood steering in an exposed fashion.*

Above: The rear of the fuel tank carries model identification on the early Model As.

Top Right: Steel spokes with a round profile carry the dual tricycle front wheels and are wrapped in 5.50-16-inch rubber.

Right: A 975-rpm PTO shaft makes for a powerful method of delivering energy to any Model A accessories.

the center of each wheel, dimensions of 56-72 inches could be set to best suit the crops being planted or harvested.

The Model A, in all of its variations, was seen in the John Deere sales catalog through 1952. Not only had this classic tractor endured the Great Depression, it actually came through with flying colors. As always, the colors in question were green and John Deere Yellow.

The 309-cid engine with two cylinders was John Deere's mainstay for many decades.

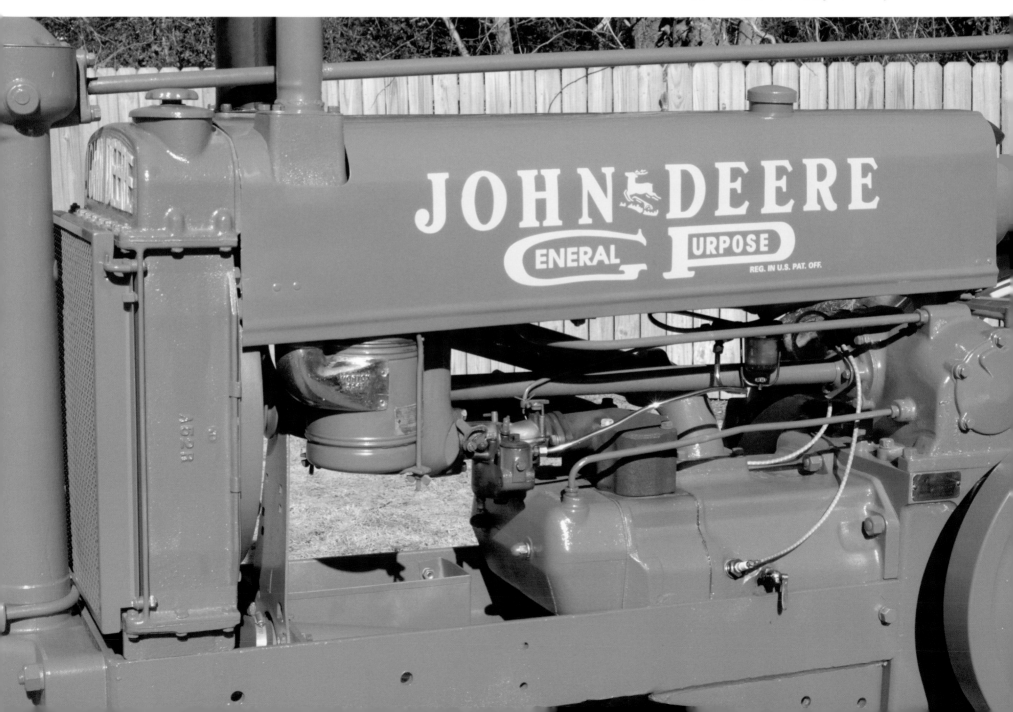

1935 Model B

The vertical ribs of a steel storage building seem to accentuate the verticalness of John Deere's product.

Several years of intense development preceded the introduction of the John Deere Model B, which took over where the GP left off. It wasn't until October 1934 that production of the Model B began, but sales would quickly reflect the years of effort that went into the design.

Oddly enough, all the time spent crafting the GP's replacement failed to reveal one chink in the B's armor. The frames of early Model Bs were formed using steel angle, welded into the required contours. The front pedestal was attached to this frame using a four-bolt pattern. Testing failed to reveal the weakness of this assembly, but actual field use quickly exposed the flaw. As sturdy as it appeared, the frame and four-bolt mounting were simply not up to the task when put to use in farming.

A little more than 2,000 Model Bs were produced using this layout, before drastic changes were made. The later units were assembled using a cast-iron frame and a much stronger eight-bolt pedestal attachment. After the initial stumble and alteration, the Model B went on to become one of the most successful John Deere tractors ever produced.

The standard configuration for the B included dual front "tricycle" wheels. These could be of all-steel construction or steel with rubber tires mounted. When buying a Model B with rubber tires, a set of 5.00-15 "donuts" were wrapped around the steel rims. This 1935 unit features the round-spoke wheels at all four corners.

A 149-cid kerosene fed, two-cylinder engine provided the Model B with motivation. A Marvel-Schebler carburetor was used to dole out the fuel sparingly. Good economy was one of the selling points of the Model B. Four forward speeds allowed the B to reach 5.25 mph and a single reverse gear provided a rate of 3.75 mph of terminal velocity. When shipped, the 3,275-pound B measured 120.5 inches in length and stood 56 inches tall at the radiator.

Deere & Co. would go on to deliver the Model B in a variety of configurations to meet the needs of almost any farming operation. When first produced, the B sold for as little as $600, but by the end of its run in 1952, both the tractor's abilities and its cost had risen. A 1952 edition would cost as much as $2,100. Yet, with overall production totaling more than 300,000 units, the B proved to be a worthy tractor.

Despite the weakness of the four-bolt design, or perhaps because of it, collectors covet every opportunity to include early Model Bs in their collections. Of the many Deere tractors in his personal collection, Duane Schlomann considers himself lucky to have this rare unit as part of his holdings. It has the optional rear fenders, which add some value and desirability.

Of the many Deere tractors in his personal collection, Duane Schlomann considers himself lucky to have this rare general-purpose tractor as part of his holdings.

▲ A heavy spring is the only comfort allowed the pilot. The foot pedals are within easy reach of a farmer seated in the saddle-type steel seat.

◀ This Model B marking appears on the rear face of the gas tank.

Above: With stylish sheet metal still years in the future, the over-engine steering apparatus was left exposed for all of the world to see.

Top Right: Early Model Bs had this four-bolt mounting for the pedestal but would later be upgraded to a stronger eight-bolt design with a cast-iron frame.

Right: The large diameter steering wheel provided plenty of grip as the B was muscled around the field.

◀ *The tubular profile of its wheel spokes make this Model B a shining example of what a classic 1935 Deere should look like.*

▼ *Cast directly into the legs of the rear axle, the "John Deere" name was a prominent attraction.*

1935 Model B

Far and Lower Right: This 149-cid two-cylinder engine served the Model B very well.

Opposite Page:: Even the rear axle of this Model B carried the "John Deere" name on it.

Below: Either 7.50-inch or 9.00-inch rubber could be selected when equipping your John Deere Model B, unless you preferred the all steel wheels which were still available.

1935 Model BW

The "W" in BW indicated the wide front end that reduced the number of trails left in the soil.

The Model B and some of its variants were first sold in 1934, as 1935 models. Despite the harsh reality of being introduced during the Great Depression, the Model B went on to become John Deere's best-selling tractor. The GP that came before it was a model that failed to live up to Deere's expectations, inspiring the company to draw up replacement models to fill the slot. Two new tractor designs were introduced, with the Model A coming first. It was followed very quickly by the Model B.

The offerings of the other makers were beginning to impact John Deere sales, so new John Deere products had to be something special to make up for sales lost by the GP. By the end of 1933, seven prototypes of the Model B had been assembled. Each made a strong impression on management. The first seven "test mules" were followed by another seven. Each of these tractors brandished additional improvements and grew closer to the final product. October 1934 finally saw the first copies of the Model B roll off the assembly line. They met with the approval of Deere and its fervent customer base.

With frugality in mind, the B was designed to run on cost-effective kerosene and to perform with "the power of six good horses." Of course, it didn't need a break like its equine partners. The rating of the B was limited to a single 16-inch plow in its basic row-crop setup. Variations are the spice of John Deere life and the first of these was the adaptation of the single-front-wheel BN

model. Built with California vegetable farmers in mind, the solo-wheel model would become known as the B Garden Tractor.

On the wheels of that version came the BW, which we see here. Its wide front end could be adjusted to match the track of the rear axle, thus reducing the quantity of trails left in the soil. Early examples of the BW had tread-adjustment hardware that left a lot to be desired. A better method to make adjustments was implemented after serial number 8973.

Further adaptations were done as the Model B was modified for a variety of specific farming chores.

In the '30s, new farm tractors seldom wore superfluous trim or sheet metal. These plain tractors — called unstyled models — were simply seen as tools of the trade and never felt a stylist's touch. One man who saw a need for change was industrial designer Henry Dreyfuss. He had devised many ways to dress up everyday items to add to their appeal and improve their function.

John Deere hired Dreyfuss as a consultant to review the Model B and see what he could do for the otherwise utilitarian tractor. Shortly after his arrival at the Waterloo plant, Dreyfuss drafted some ideas he thought might add beauty to the B as well as enhance its performance.

John Deere's 1939 models adopted the sleek bodywork that Dreyfuss created and sales took an immediate jump. It seemed that many buyers — even some who viewed their Model Bs as

John Deere hired Dreyfuss as a consultant to review the Model B and see what he could do for the otherwise utilitarian tractor.

JOHN DEERE
GENERAL PURPOSE
REG. U.S. PAT. OFF.

▲ Maximum belt horsepower for the 1935 Model B was listed as 15.07. It would increase as the dimension of the engine grew throughout the years.

◄ The rear of the unstyled tank also carried the Deere name as a constant reminder to the rider settled into the seat, driving a Model B.

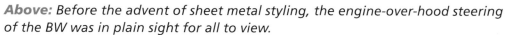

Above: Before the advent of sheet metal styling, the engine-over-hood steering of the BW was in plain sight for all to view.

Top Right: The BW featured a front axle whose width was adjustable and the adjustment could be achieved using the hardware shown here.

Right: As was typically the case with John Deere tractors, the seat post wore the model name in yellow.

Far Left: When so equipped, the front axle of the BW could be adjusted to match the tread-width of the rear tires.

Left: A maximum of 1,728 feet could be pulled by the hitch on the 1935 Model B, but that number would also grow as larger-displacement engines were brought out.

JOHN DEERE
GENERAL PURPOSE

From 1935-1938, this 149-cid two-cylinder engine served the Model B very well.

Right: These 48 x 5.25-inch steel rims featured round spokes and were wrapped with rubber tires, which were optional.

Above: Always proud to display the brand, the John Deere name was prominently cast into the "legs" of the rear axle.

farm tools — liked it better when their equipment had some panache.

This 1935 Model BW has been fitted with round spoke wheels at all four corners. They are considered a special feature of this tractor. From 1935-1940, the Model B was shifted with a transmission that carried four forward gears and a single reverse. From 1941 to the end of the series in 1952, two additional forward speeds were added. The 3,200-pound Model B sold for $600-$900, depending on which version was chosen and how it was equipped. Tires were either of the all-steel variety or of the more flexible rubber-type that was growing in popularity.

In all of its forms and throughout the entire production run, the Model B would go on to sell in numbers totaling more than 300,000.

The John Deere BW was fitted with spoke wheels at all corners – painted bright yellow, of course.

Although two years away from the sleeker "styled" units, the Model B John Deere was considered a workhorse around the farm.

As fans of the John Deere tractor know, 1937 was to be the penultimate year for the unstyled models. Henry Dreyfuss and Associates had already been employed to create some new style for the line, but the 1937-1938 models would remain unstyled tractors in the barest of work clothes.

The Model B first saw production in 1935. It was based on the Model A, which had been released a year earlier. By using the platform and parameters of the A, the B came to be a slightly smaller variation of the same tractor. The Model B was more than a foot shorter in length and stood nine inches shorter at the hood than its sibling. A weight savings of more than 500 pounds was realized, making the Model B a more nimble tractor. The cylinder displacement of the two engines was vastly different. The 1934-1939 Model A engine had 309 cubic inches. The 1934-1938 Model B engine had only 149 cubic inches.

This difference in displacement did little to dissuade buyers from signing up as Model B owners and this tractor became one of the best-selling John Deere tractors in history. Perhaps the price difference told the tale. The Model A sold for $1,050, while a Model B of the same vintage could be had for anywhere from $600-$850.

The B was available in your choice of all-fuel or gasoline variations. It offered a myriad of front-axle styles. Even a crawler was built using the BO/BR variations of the B. The example pictured here wears dual tricycle wheels. As witnessed by the eight-bolt pedestal, it was a late-production unit. Early Model Bs wore only four bolts at the same mounting point. Problems using the four-bolt design in actual farming operations soon forced the change to the eight-bolt design.

The long hood of the B was fairly simple in design. It had a square profile and little if anything in the way of fashion. This would be rectified after the 1939 models were massaged by Dreyfuss and his team.

The Model B's steering arm ran exposed over the length of the hood and culminated at the junction box that led to the front wheels. There was nothing pretty about this arrangement, but its durability was legendary. Seating was still the contoured steel bucket complete with perforations for drainage, but nothing else. No one said the early days of farming were comfortable.

Round spoke wheels are seen under each rubber donut on this tractor, but other Model Bs may mount a mix of solid and spoke rims. Early examples of the Model B used 10-spline axles to drive the rear wheels, while the BWH and BNH versions received 12-spline axles. Bs built after serial number 6000 carried 12-splines. Others had 15-spline axles. With the axle splines in charge of handling the power delivered to the wheels, designs with more splines provide better strength, as long as the splines don't become too thin in the process.

The rear axle was splined to deliver power to the rear wheel of the John Deere Model B.

▲ One change that
occurred quickly after
the first Bs took to the
fields was the addition
of four more bolts
to the pedestal. This
strengthened a key
structural aspect of
the tractor.

◄ The dual-tricycle-
wheel option was one
of many seen on the
Model B and, perhaps,
the most commonly-
selected one.

▲ *One advantage to the slab sides of the Model B's hood was the ability to place easy- to-read logo identification on the flanks of the tractor.*

◄ *The Model B's over-the-engine steering mechanism terminated at the junction box. The box then directed input, vertically, to the wheels.*

▶ "Home sweet home" — at least out in the fields! The steel bucket seat was all the operator had to rest his "laurels" in during stints behind the wheel working crops.

The design, layout and ruggedness of the Model B resulted in more than 320,000 copies being built during this model's lifetime.

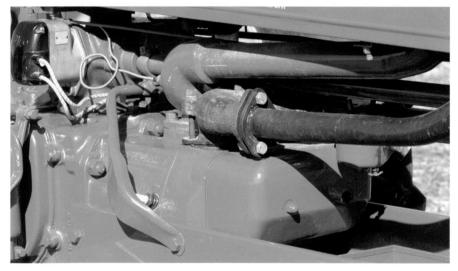

Far Left: Being from the unstyled era, very little beautification was found on the first Model Bs.

Far Bottom Left: Displacing 149 cubic inches when first introduced, the Model B's two-cylinder engine would grow to 190.4 cid, before production ended in 1952.

Left: Round spokes made of steel hold the large wheel rims in place on this tractor. Other versions of the Model B were built using a solid steel wheel.

The frame of the 1937 Model B was also lengthened by five inches to more easily accommodate the use of front-mounted cultivators. This alteration did not occur until after serial number 42200, making the later versions "long-frame" Bs.

Available options on the Model B included a hydraulic lift, electric lighting and a rear-mounted PTO or power take-off.

The design, layout and ruggedness of the Model B resulted in more than 320,000 copies being built during this model's lifetime. With roots going back to 1935, the final Model Bs wouldn't roll off the assembly line until 1952. Although introduced during the Depression, the John Deere Model B persevered and went on to carve a solid notch in Deere's belt of success.

Along with refreshing new bodywork displacement of the two-cylinder engine increased to 174.9 cubic inches.

Once John Deere had overcome and corrected problems related to the four-bolt steering pedestal clamp of the 1935 Model Bs, tractors with replacement eight-bolt clamps became one of the company's best sellers. In 1937, Henry Dreyfuss also added his styling genius to the line, by showing everyone what he could do with a farm tractor. In little more than a year, the newly-styled Model A and Model B were ready for the marketplace. They were released as 1939 models.

The success of the revised B was almost immediate. The tractor was popular even in its unstyled configuration. The addition of a sleek grille wrap and hood designed by Dreyfuss propelled the latest models to the next level. As with any proper design, the sheet metal changes added some functionality, too. The grille helped to keep foreign matter from getting lodged in the radiator. A reduced-width hood allowed for better viewing of any cultivators mounted beneath the frame.

Along with the refreshing new bodywork came some mechanical upgrades. The twin-cylinder engine had its displacement increased to 174.9 cubic inches, which raised output for the Model B. Overall length of the 1939 B was also increased by five inches, but that was due primarily to the new sheet metal. The cost of the 1939 models also saw a rise to $1,000-$1,500, depending on equipment.

With every boost in power, farmers sought new ways to put their John Deere tractors to use. One of the more common dilemmas facing farm operators was devising a simple method of moving animal waste that accumulated during the winter months. To tackle this problem mechanically, John Deere introduced its own rear-mounted loader in 1939. When attached to the rear end of the Model B, it provided a far more efficient method of moving the stockpiled manure.

Operation of the loader was accomplished through a series of cables, chains and clutches. Once in position, the farmer would rotate the seat of his Model B 180 degrees to face the mound in question. Powered by the Model B's PTO, the loader became a handy device. Using foot and hand levers, the offensive material could easily be loaded into a horse-drawn spreader. When in the hands of an experienced operator, the loader mechanism was capable of keeping a trio of horse-drawn wagons busy.

The 1939 Model B remained largely unchanged until 1947. The sales catalog released that year showed that some incremental alterations had been made to the wildly-successful Model B. The availability of powered and non-powered accessories would be quickly expanded, as farmers seemed anxious to find new ways to automate operations previously done by manual methods.

The farmer could rotate the seat 180 degrees and operate the loader via a series of cables, chains and clutches.

▲ *A pair of wheels of "tricycle" format were common on the Model B, but other variations were available.*

◄ *When the John Deere Model B was equipped with a rear-mounted loader or similar device, a front-mounted counterweight provided better overall balance.*

Left: Steel spoke wheels were ensconced with the tractor owner's choice of available tires. Each tire design was suited to specific farming conditions.

Above: Some things never changed, like the practice of stamping the model name of the tractor onto the seat post.

Opposite: The two-cylinder engine beneath the freshly-styled hood had a larger cylinder displacement that allowed the tractor to handle additional duties.

Far Left: The steel tines of the rear-mounted loader on this John Deere Model B are capable of grabbing far more material in a single pass than a farmer with a pitchfork.

Left: The revisions to the design of the Model Bs body didn't affect every facet of the tractor, as you can tell when you see this carryover-type steering wheel.

Above: The intake and exhaust stacks exited from the smooth new hood and helped the engine breathe.

Left: Mounted to the rear of this Model B is a manure loader. It allowed farmers to quickly transfer a winter's worth of waste into their manure spreaders with far less effort.

Above: The new sheet metal of the Henry Dreyfuss-styled 1939 John Deere models provided a sleeker, better-looking environment for the gauges.

Left: This 1939 John Deere Model B has rubber tires mounted on steel spoke wheels.

The newly styled models from John Deere were an immediate success.

The introduction of the John Deere Model A tractor in 1934 would prove to be a pivotal decision for John Deere. With America still firmly in the grasp of the Great Depression, business was hardly robust for manufacturing firms. Even this fact didn't change the truth that the competition was greatly outselling John Deere products. With new-equipment sales down across the board, the John Deere Tractor Company could hardly afford to be the "smallest fish in the pond." Knowing that corporate survival would be based on sales of future tractors, in 1931, the company began research and development work on what would soon become the John Deere Model A.

Prototype Model As were designated by the letters FX. These tractors were assembled using Deere's proven two-cylinder layout. Since economic conditions weren't great, the tractor maker had no desire to "re-invent the wheel." The first test mules for the Model A carried a 30-hp engine, although Deere had plans to use a 24-hp power plant in production versions of the new and larger tractor. Testing rolled on and, by 1933, Deere engineers were ready to go to the next phase of development. This would entail the manufacturing of 10 near-production-specification tractors. These "AA" units suffered from some initial "teething" problems, but, by March 1934, Deere was ready to sell the Model A to the public.

Early copies of the Model A were of the unstyled type that was common in the tractor industry in 1934. Although lacking any decorative sheet metal, they could be had in numerous variations, depending on the farmer's requirements. The goal was to provide a tractor for all seasons, so that its sales could overtake those of the competitors that John Deere had fallen behind.

One of the most important options on the new Model A was a hydraulic lift. The mechanical device seen earlier in these pages worked well, but usually dropped the device being used with a solid thud. With hydraulics, the lift could be eased to the ground. This would add life to an implement, since hydraulic operation would be like handling it with kid gloves. This tractor has hydraulics, as well as an optional Behlen overdrive that adds two more forward gears.

Even with all the efforts of Deere to produce a terrific new tractor for the agricultural mass market, some minor flaws arose in early Model As. A revised method of mounting the rear fenders and a relocated fuel cap were among the small changes required to make the Model A the best John Deere tractor ever offered. When farmers bought a rubber-tire version of the Model A, the steel wheels were changed from the spoked type to a pressed type. In addition, as production continued, radiator shutters replaced the previous radiator curtain device.

The biggest change on the 1939 tractors was styling. With the sheet metal crafted by industrial designer Henry Dreyfuss, these more-elegant-looking John Deere models were an immediate hit. However, sales continued to falter. Nearly 500 unsold Model As

Henry Dreyfuss was hired to breathe new life into the Deere catalog and the 1939 models were the first to roll off the line.

JOHN DEERE

▲ Dual tricycle wheels were but one of the many options offered to the Model A buyer. Options like this helped widen the appeal of the John Deere tractors by satisfying every faction in the marketplace.

◄ A large-diameter steering wheel was provided to navigate the Model A through farmyards and fields.

Above: The Model A was given new life in 1939 as the first of the styled units were sold.

Top Right: The rear axle of the Model A was designed with provisions for adjusting axle width and provided farmers with a variety of options to meet changing needs.

Right: The fenders were bolted to the rear axle and provided a high degree of protection from flying debris during operation of the tractor.

were returned to the factory to be retro-fitted with the new sheet metal. Deere had hopes that they would sell with the updated sheet metal. The retro-fitted A and B models were little changed beneath their fancy new "duds." This made sense. After spending so much time and effort creating the Model A, Deere engineers knew that the tractors did not need a lot of mechanical changes.

As stated earlier in this book, the manufacturer's suggested retail price for 1934-1940 Model As was $1,050. That went up to $2,400 for the 1941-1952 versions. Once the initial issues were addressed and corrected, the Model A became very popular and helped bring the John Deere Tractor Company back from the brink of failure. It became one of the company's most popular designs.

Due to budgetary constraints, designers of the Model A stuck with a two-cylinder engine. However, the power level was increased over previous two-cylinder models.

1939 Model H

The 1939 John Deere Model H came with dual-tricycle front tires.

By the late-1930s, many farming operations were getting big enough to think about discontinuing the use of horses, although they were too small to afford a tractor. John Deere had an answer to this dilemma: "Sell your four-legged power to pay for a new John Deere tractor." This convinced many American farmers to take a leap of faith. Of course, the perfect tractor had to be able to do a wide array of tasks economically and, because the small farms of the day often encompassed nearly 100 acres of land, the tractor couldn't be too small, either.

To address this conundrum, John Deere created the Model H. It was in 1937 that plans for the Model H were initiated. Guidelines for the tractor were given to the John Deere Tractor Company's research and development department. They included low cost and high efficiency to break through the small farmer's buying resistance.

Although the new tractor could not require a huge investment to purchase it, the machine would also have to be adaptable to almost any type of farming being done at the time. With these thoughts in mind, design work on such a tractor – which ultimately became the Model H — was set into motion. Prototype models were code-named "OX" and tractors with the numbers 138-143 were built for testing purposes. By model-year 1939, this phase of the project was completed and the Model H was readied for sale.

Power for this compact-size tractor was derived from a 99.7-cid, two-cylinder engine took output from the camshaft, instead of the crankshaft (as was typical on bigger tractors). Cost savings were achieved by the elimination of added gearing for the final drive. The high cost of adding a road-use gear was also eliminated through the use of a governed over-ride pedal. When top gear was selected, 1,800 rpm was attainable. This translated into almost two more miles per hour for road use.

All this was achieved while retaining designed-in high-mileage limits. A total of three forward gears and one reverse gear were encased in the gearbox. The Model H had a top speed of 7-1/2 mph.

The Model H came with Deere's dual-tricycle front tires, but other variations were optional. A single front wheel was seen on the HN model and a high-clearance single front wheel was a feature of the HNH. The HW and HWH models both included an adjustable front axle, which was of the high-clearance type in one case. Overall length of the Model H was just 112-1/2 inches. The height of the tractor, to the top of the radiator cap, was only 52-1/2 inches. As far as shipping weight, the diminutive H tipped the scale at just over a ton, when equipped with four-ply tires.

Keeping the engine from overheating was John Deere's thermo-siphon cooling system, which circulated 5-1/2 gallons of fluid. The tractor's "distillate" or all-fuel system included two fuel tanks. There was a small 7/8-gallon tank for gasoline and a

Depending on options, the Model H pricest ranged from $595-$650

▲ Unlike automobile clutches encased in the transmission housing, the clutches on John Deere tractors are externally-mounted mechanisms.

◀ Selection of one of the three forward gears or the single reverse gear was achieved with this lever and a foot-operated clutch.

Above: Holding the steering wheel firmly in place is this steel tube. It is attached directly to the "bedrock" chassis of the Model H.

Left: The early use of styled sheet metal on John Deere tractors is reflected by the design of this 1939 Model H.

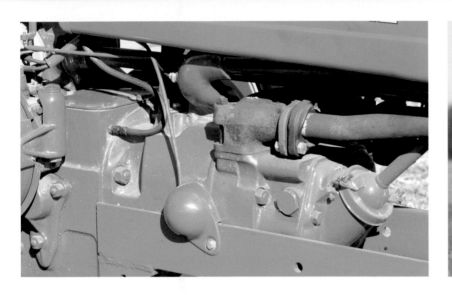

Far Left: Displacing just under 100 inches and fed by distillates, the two-cylinder Model H engine delivers enough power to propel the tractor to a top speed of 7-1/2 mph.

Left: This large-diameter wheel provided plenty of the leverage needed to steer the John Deere Model H tractor around a farm.

This Model H has steel rear wheels with ribbed rubber tires.

The height of the tractor, to the top of the radiator cap, was only 52-1/2 inches.

7-1/2 gallon tank for fuel.

When purchased new, the Model H carried a price tag that ranged from $595-$650, depending on how it was equipped. Production ran from 1939-1947 and nearly 59,000 copies rolled off the assembly line in Waterloo, Iowa.

The current owner bought this example of the John Deere Model H years ago at the urging of his ex-domestic partner.

Typical of the period this tractor was built in is a steering mechanism that makes a long, fully-exposed run to the front pedestal.

Many of us regret decisions made with people from our past, but despite a required trip to Montana, the purchase of this tractor and another one set his hobby activities into motion. The ex- has moved on, but this collector's first John Deere restoration has stayed with him to this day. 🦌

The styled versions of the Model A were 10 inches longer than unstyled versions.

As we learned earlier in this book, in 1934, the John Deere Model A was developed to take the place of the C/GP tractor, which had not been as warmly received as the John Deere Tractor Company had hoped it would be. While the new model was being designed, a laundry list of updates was created to insure that it sold better. Once released, it lasted 20 years. However, since the tractor marketplace was always demanding changes, many revisions to the design were needed over the years.

After Henry Dreyfuss modernized the 1939 Model A, sales of his styled version flourished, proving that the famous industrial designer's blending of form and function really worked. Increasing demands put on the popular tractor resulted in a 1940 displacement boost from 309 to 321 cubic inches. The larger — and more powerful — engine was mated to a larger-diameter PTO shaft and delivered higher output. Growing from 1.125 inches to 1.375 inches in diameter, the new PTO shaft became the standard of the industry. A rated speed of 975 rpm was seen on all versions of the Model A, when measured at the PTO shaft.

Added ease of use could be achieved by ordering an all-new electric-start option for the 1940 Model A. Horsepower at the belt drive would increase slightly with each new version of the Model A. On the first tractors in 1934, the rating was 24.71 hp. This grew to 36.13 hp on later editions. And it seemed that, regardless of how much power was added to each new model, farmers wanted and needed more.

The styled versions of the Model A were 10 inches longer than the older plain-Jane versions they replaced. They also carried an additional 500 pounds of weight due to added equipment features and sheet metal. Since there was a price to be paid for progress and beauty, after 1941 the tractors sold for $1,350 more than they had before.

The rubber-tired 1941 model featured six forward speeds, up from four in previous tractors. Only one reverse gear was available, of course, as it had been from the start. After World War II erupted, very few changes were made to the Model A until 1948 editions started to roll off the assembly line.

The 1943 Model A seen here had all the changes adopted in 1941. This tractor was delivered to the Piper Brothers John Deere dealership in Tennessee. It originally wore steel wheels at all four corners. The father of the current owner bought it from the first owner in the 1960s and, later, sold it to a friend. That friend used the A for active farming for 36 years.

After this lengthy period of daily field activity, the tractor sat for several years and caught some much-needed rest. Now, it is owned by a gentleman who took possession of it in 2000. He then set out to restore the tired tractor to factory-fresh condition. Four months were needed to bring it back to life. When the restoration was in process, rubber tires were added to boost the tractor's use in local parades and events. The older steel wheels made a real mess of pavement and took a beating themselves when traveling over concrete or blacktop surfaces.

This 1943 John Deere styled Model A
has the longer 6-3/4-inch engine stroke
first adopted in 1941.

JOHN DEERE

▲ The Model A's two-cylinder engine grew from 309 cid to 321 cid in 1941 and stayed at this displacement for 1943. This one is a gasoline-fed version.

◀ As you can see here, early John Deere tractors had little in the way of instrumentation. This 1943 Model A uses a simple two-gauge array.

Above: *The styled version of the John Deere Model A sports this curvaceous sheet metal at the nose to hide the square-edged radiator lurking underneath.*

Top Right: *This steel plate was used when hanging a front-mounted cultivator, a popular farming option.*

Right: *Model designations moved around on early John Deere tractors. It was painted on the seat post on 1943 models.*

This tractor originally had steel wheels, but during its restoration rubber tires were installed so it was suitable for driving on paved roads.

The Lindeman brothers had experience building crawlers and could see that it would be simple to fit John Deere tractors with steel tracks.

The John Deere Tractor Company had a reputation for building tractors that could be used in almost any type of farming operation. However, one of the John Deere tractor's weaknesses was its use in orchards with sandy soil. All tractors running on tires had trouble getting traction in sand. Steering a tractor in sand was also a challenge.

Seeking a solution to this dilemma, Jesse Lindeman and his three brothers devised a way to mount tracks, like those used on army tanks, to a John Deere chassis. They initially tried this on a GP model, but didn't really perfect the technology until they used a John Deere Model BO tractor as the basis for their crawler-tread conversion.

Lindeman and his three brothers grew experienced in building crawlers. When Jesse first saw the John Deere chassis, he immediately grasped how easy it would be to alter the existing frame to carry heavy steel tracks and make a functioning crawler. From 1939-1946, Lindeman Power Equipment Company converted a number of BO tractors into crawlers. However, with the BO model about to be phased out in 1947, they could see the writing on the wall.

At that time, the John Deere Tractor Company approached Lindeman Power Equipment Company about doing the same type of conversion to a new model that they were developing. Jesse Lindeman said he had a better idea and offered to sell the firm to Deere. A deal was struck and, on January 1, 1947, John Deere took possession of the Lindeman Power Equipment Company operation.

Since Lindeman Power Equipment Company was located in Yakima, Washington, the process of shipping components and finished tractors between there and the new John Deere plant in Dubuque, Iowa, became a real chore. So, in 1954, Deere relocated the Lindeman Brothers operation in Dubuque to consolidate the manufacturing process.

The BO that Lindeman started with evolved from the Model B, which first appeared in 1935. The BO was designed as an orchard tractor. It was modeled on the John Deere BR, but featured differential braking, instead of a service brake like early BRs (later BRs could be ordered with the differential brake).

Power for 1946 Model Bs (all variations) came from a 174.9-cid two-cylinder engine that was available with all-fuel or gasoline options. Six forward gears and a single reverse were provided. Prices for the BR and BO ranged from $700-$900 as delivered from Deere. Adding the Lindeman crawler conversion raised the total cost to $1,360. Early versions of the crawler had their track assemblies cast at the Lindeman Power Equipment Company factory, but improved castings resulted when Deere switched to a foundry in Pittsburgh.

Like all American manufacturers, Deere had a tough time getting raw materials during World War II. Many materials were

"John Deere" was printed on the hood and "Lindeman" was on the side covers.

▲ Another feature Lindeman Power Equipment Company carried over from the John Deere BO was the sheet metal hood and fuel storage tank.

◄ These springs attached to the crawler helped soak up the irregularities of orchard-type terrains. They helped smooth out the ride and kept the tracks tight against the drive sprockets.

Above: This Lindeman crawler was based on the John Deere Model BO tractor and used that model's 174.9-cid two-cylinder engine.

Top Right: Starting the engine on most early John Deere tractors required turning this massive flywheel by hand, until the engine coughed to life.

Right: An external clutch was employed on the Lindeman-converted BO, although belt-driven accessories were not as common on the crawlers.

Far Left: The John Deere name was still cast into the front of the radiator housing on 1946 models. It certainly made a strong statement about who the manufacturer was.

Left: Improved handling was achieved with the Lindeman conversion, but operator comfort remained low on the list of priorities.

The two-cylinder engine of the BO displaced 174.9 inches and proved to be an adequate power plant whether the tractor rolled on tires or tracks.

A PTO was provided at the rear of the crawler to power accessories. A rat's nest of control arms was required to operate all the functions of Lindeman Crawlers and a skilled hand was a necessity.

The steel tracks on this conversion were fitted with rubber pads that allowed it to be used on paved surfaces. These were also used on U.S. Navy crawlers during World War II.

deemed too important to be consumed by civilian production. So, when a dozen copies of the Lindeman crawler were built for wartime use by the U.S. Navy, it helped Deere get the steel it needed to continue other production. The U.S. Navy models of this tractor had rubber pads on the steel tracks and were used on the docks where naval ships were serviced.

In 1947, the Model M replaced the BO for crawler conversions. It was modified and became the Model MC in 1949. Postwar improvements in rubber-tired tractors eliminated many benefits of the Lindeman crawler. However, until the time that this change took place, the crawler could not be beaten when it came to use in the hilly and loosely-soiled terrain of most orchards.

This tractor is fitted with a rear light to make nighttime farming safer and more convenient.

Randy Germany's first exposure to the John Deere Model G tractor was in a local "boneyard." He later saw one entered in a tractor-pulling contest. Then, he decided to find one for his own collection of "Letter" models. This 1951 was brought to Tennessee from Oklahoma. Randy purchased the tractor and restored it with support from his understanding family.

Sandwiched between the pain of the Great Depression and the approach of World War II, the United States was far from being in peak economic condition when Deere & Company started to grow its line of successful tractors. The Model D, introduced in 1923, trundled along in sales. It performed well, but buyers wanted the power of the D in a lighter tractor so more of the engine's output could be put to good use.

The Model G was rolled out for 1937 and proved to be a highly-capable tractor that weighed half a ton less than the D. John Deere had already used the letters A, B, C, D and GP to identify different models, so F seemed the next logical choice for a new tractor. To avoid confusion in the market, that letter was skipped and a G designation was applied. The Model G was powerful enough to carry a trio of 14-inch plow bottoms, a 28-inch thresher or four-row devices with ease. The four-speed gearbox was shifted with a single handle, versus the two required on previous models. Six speeds were on tap on the later Model Gs.

Powering the G was a 412.5-cid two-cylinder engine fired by distillates. Early production models were built using a shorter radiator, but it was soon blamed for excessive temperatures. Deere offered buyers a taller radiator as a replacement, so the short-radiator tractors are a rare sight today. The offering of tractors in a number of wheel combinations continued to be popular and the G came in a variety of formats.

Like most tractors of their era, early Model Gs were not styled, but the introduction of the red International Harvester M model cast the Model G into the shadows. It would take several years, but in 1942 the John Deere Model G was finally upgraded with sleek new bodywork and returned to tractor buyers. One downside for Deere and Company was that the bodywork added to the cost of building tractors.

During World War II, the U.S. Government instituted wage-and-price controls to stabilize the economy. Despite the fact that the styled G cost more to build, Deere was not allowed to increase the selling prices on existing models. To get around this, the company offered a modified version of the tractor, which could then be sold for a higher price. This GM version was sold carrying a slightly higher price tag to improve the company's bottom line. World War II ended in 1945 and Deere renamed the GM the G. The year 1947 saw the Roll-O-Matic front axle added to options list.

Styled Model Gs were seen in 1947, since continuing improvements were made to keep this tractor competitive. The

A yellow "G" appeared in a black circle on the sides of the styled radiator.

JOHN DEERE

▲ More than 36 belt horsepower was available from the Model G when a belt was attached to the spinning clutch drum. The PTO could be used to power a variety of implements.

◀ The later styled versions of the Model G had a comfortable padded bench seat that supplanted the steel bucket seat used on early John Deere tractors.

Above: Rated at 975 rpm, the Model G's PTO was up to most tasks that involved powered accessories.

Right: Intake and exhaust stacks emanating from the styled hood of the Model G stood tall.

Far Left: A vertical stack of gauges kept the operator informed about oil and water pressure as well as the amperes being drawn.

Left: The 1947 model year brought the addition of the Roll-O-Matic front axle to the Model G's option list.

The 1951 Model G was started with a gas engine, then switched over to distillates during operation. It used six forward ratios in its gearbox.

JOHN DEERE

Powering the G was a 412.5-cid two-cylinder engine fired by distillates.

Top: John Deere's Powr-Trol hydraulic system was available before the 1951 models were released and continued to be offered after the Model G went out of production.

Above: Adjustable for widths between 60- 84 inches, the rear axle of the Model G could be adapted to suit the changing needs of farmers.

Left: The 412.5-cid two-cylinder engine in the Model G employed overhead valves for efficient breathing.

latest alteration was the use of a padded seat in place of the steel bucket-type seat. The new seat design meant that the "G" designation had to be moved from the seat post to the front of the hood. Deere added their Powr-Trol hydraulics after that and in 1951 a high-crop adaptation was seen. A constant flow of upgrades for the G were well received and it would survive into the 1953 model year, eclipsing the loss of its smaller A and B siblings.

A collector bought this tractor in 2002 and after having problems with the engine, he restored it completely two years later.

After World War II, the John Deere Tractor Company experienced disappointing sales of its Model GP tractor. In addition, the company saw economic turmoil throughout the world. It was clear that the firm needed a new tractor to survive and some amount of thought was given to making a completely new product. However, common sense and financial restraints dictated a design more like those that sold well in the past.

In 1931, plans to create the replacement for the four-year-old GP were launched. Various pre-production machines were built and tested before John Deere introduced the Model A in March 1934. The first Model A off the assembly line had carried serial number 410012. The early Model As were unstyled tractors, but starting in 1938, the versions styled by Henry Dreyfuss arrived and gained instant buyer acceptance.

In 1940, the Model A's spec engine displacement grew to 321 cubic inches from 309 cubic inches and electric starting was adopted. The hood had to be changed to accommodate the battery and these models became known as "slant-dash" models. Starting in 1941, Model As fitted with rubber tires had a six-speed gearbox thrown into the mix. A few additional alterations were seen later in the '40s.

In 1947, dealers received the latest Model A. It implemented an improved chassis layout and was called the "Late-Styled A." Having honed and enhanced the already popular A for half a dozen years, John Deere had a runaway winner on its roster. The Model A

production plant was pushed to near capacity as tractor operators snapped up the newest iteration. A few minor revisions were again made for the 1949 models. They included a single gearshift lever and a lower-speed creeper gear.

As with most John Deere tractors, the Model A could be purchased in several configurations to suit different purposes. The 1952 model we see here was destined for use on the West Coast and has Deere's "California conversion." Besides being built as a high-crop tractor, this one has an additional 10-inch spacer installed between the rear axle and the drop housing. This modification protected Gladiola crops from being bruised by the drop housing as it passed over the rows of flowers.

This version of the Model A is seldom seen in the Midwest. In 1989, it was brought to Iowa by a collector. The current owner bought the Model A in 2002. A mishap with the engine prompted a complete restoration in 2004. This project involved the replacement of many internal components, as well as fresh sheet metal, and resulted in what is basically a "new" tractor. The high-crop Model A was always of interest to Duane Schlomann and his grandson Brett. They were excited to finally be able to add one to their collection.

This 1952 Model A General Purpose (GP) comes from the final year of production for this model. While the price of this tractor had climbed from $1,050 in 1934 to $2,400 in 1952, it was still a proven design and one of the most successful units ever offered by the John Deere Tractor Company.

1952 Model A High-Crop

This tractor has an extra spacer installed between the rear axle and drop housing, a modification that kept gladiolas safe as the John Deere passed over them.

▲ John Deere tractors used external clutches to moderate speed once the farmer selected a certain drive gear.

◄ The overall height of the high-crop tractor required adding these steel step plates for easy access to the pillion and controls.

Right: While the first Model A units were unstyled and the lacked the designer's touch, later units carried sleekly-styled sheet metal that immediately boosted sales.

Lower Left: For high-crop farming, the front axle provided added clearance. It width could be adjusted from 60-84 inches to provide a custom fit for the type of crop being farmed.

Lower Right: Designed to make tractors suitable for cultivating and harvesting tall crops, the high-crop option provided plenty of clearance from the front axle rearward.

Far Left: A trio of gauges kept the operator informed about the operating condition of his tractor as he worked the fields.

Right: John Deere's Powr-Trol hydraulic system gave the operator a wide array of choices when attaching accessories to the rear of the tractor.

Below: From 1940 until the end of Model A production in 1952, a 321-cid engine replaced the earlier 309-cid unit. After 1941, the rubber-tired Model A could be ordered with a six-speed gearbox.

1952 Model G

Model Gs of the '50s had styled sheet metal and electric start as standard fare.

The John Deere Model G tractor had a long and productive life. Its production run began in 1937 and went all the way to 1953. It was originally designed to match the power of the Model D it replaced, although it weighed less. Using the same power unit as the D gave the G a better power-to-weight ratio and made it more potent and efficient.

Sold as a larger version of the Models A and B, the Model G was initially marketed as a three-plow tractor. It could pull three 14-inch plow bottoms, a 28-inch thresher or four-row implements. This made the G a versatile machine well suited to the day-to-day operations of growing farms. Adding to its flexibility, was the wide array of wheel-and-tire configurations offered for the G.

The 1952 G shown here features the three-wheeled cotton-picker layout, one of many configurations seen on the tractor's options sheet. A dual-rear-wheel arrangement was seen on a few versions of the G, but most of them carried dual tricycle wheels or a wide-front-axle setup.

The engine of the G did not change during its 16-year run, which indicated that its 412.5-cid twin was up to any task. From 1937-1941, Model Gs had only four forward gears, but two additional gears were added to Gs built after 1942. The top speed of the four-speed version was seen as 6 mph, while the six-speed editions did 12.5 mph. Only one reverse gear was used from beginning to end, but the single reverse speed increased from 3 mph in early models to 3.50 mph in the later versions. A 975-rpm PTO shaft was on call to power any implements that a farmer wished to use with his G.

Model Gs made from 1947 on had styled sheet metal on par with other "Late Styled" John Deere tractors. Electric start was also made standard equipment that year. In 1951, a high-crop option was added. For 1952, Model Gs were upgraded with Deere's Thermo-syphon system, which improved engine cooling.

Due to changes in production and model designations, there were some jumps and skips in the serial number sequence for the Model G. The first example carried serial No. 1000 and the last tractor made in 1953 had No. 64530 stamped on its identification tag. The popular Model G, which outlasted the Models A and B, was finally replaced by an even better tractor called the Model 70, which was first introduced in 1953.

For 1952 a John Deere's Thermo-Syphon system improved engine cooling.

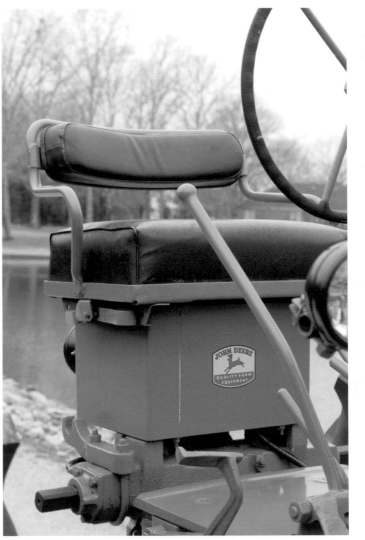

▲ *As you can see by the untouched condition of its fresh paint, the belt-drive system of this particular 1952 John Deere Model G has not been following the tractor's complete restoration.*

◀ *One improvement seen on the "Late Styled" Gs was a padded seat to replace the uncomfortable steel bucket-type seat.*

Above: The single-wheel configuration gave the Model G a trim view and provided minimal track width when put into use.

Top Right: When powered by the 975-rpm PTO, the rear-mounted hitch provided plenty of options for implement attachments.

Right: Of the Model G's many front-axle options, the single-wheel arrangement was well-suited for cotton farming.

Far Left: Circular emblems on the tractor looked attractive. They carried the "G" model designation on a field of black against the John Deere green.

Left: A splined, width-adjustable rear axle allowed farmers to adjust the track of the Model G for farming different types of crops

JOHN DEERE

The Model G's 412.5-cid two-cylinder engine delivered 975 rpm to the tractor's PTO shaft. The same engine was used from the start of production in 1937 until production closed in 1953.

1954 Model R

The Model R had a diesel engine
that could run all day long with
its 22-gallon fuel tank.

Despite its acceptance in other forms of transportation, the diesel engine was slow to catch on with tractor designers. The weight and low output of early diesels kept tractor producers at bay. By the early 1930s, a few of John Deere's competitors had placed diesel engines into their tractors. These engines proved to be economical and, when properly designed, had more than enough power for farming use. Seeing the trend, Deere began its own research into a diesel option in 1935. Five years of preliminary testing was required before the first diesel-powered Deere prototypes were created. It then took another year or so to iron out flaws in the original designs. The outbreak of World War II suppressed additional development.

In 1944, Deere's experimental MX tractor took to the fields for further testing. The tests were extended and lasted until 1947. Satisfied with the preliminary findings, the John Deere Tractor Company set out to create a new model based on what had been learned. The company's first diesel tractor, the Model R. was the result of their efforts. Completed in the latter part of 1948, the first Rs were sold as 1949 models and sales carried on until 1954.

The Model R's large 416-cid diesel was a two-cylinder horizontal L-head engine that could run all day long on the contents of a single 22-gallon fuel tank. It took some time, but Deere engineers overcame the limitations of the diesel design and pressed it into service with terrific results. To get the big diesel going, they used a smaller, 25-cid gas-fired engine. This "pony" engine was much easier to bring to life when it was cold. Once it started, it would spin the larger diesel engine to life. A six-volt battery was all that the V-4 engine required to get started and this "tag team" procedure for getting underway was a money-saving method to run a big diesel in your Model R. Using a 10-hp engine to spin the 1,000-rpm-rated diesel to life was a brilliant idea that served John Deere well.

The primary engine was linked to a five-speed gearbox that would run the R up to 11.5 mph. A single reverse gear provided a speed of 2.5 mph. The Model R's all-gear drive replaced the chain drive of the departing D and quickly outshone the earlier technology. The big R was capable of running with up to six plow bottoms compared to the Model D's four. The inclusion of hydraulics for powered implements, plus a live PTO, pushed the Model R's sales into the "win" column for Deere.

The standard tread layout could be ordered in a choice of wheat land or rice configurations and this example is of the latter version. When fitted out for use in rice and cane fields, extra shielding was supplied to protect the running gear from the excessive moisture that was common when farming those particular crops. The brake drums and wheel bearings were also

John Deere's first diesel tractor proved to be worth the wait, as it was a good one.

JOHN DEERE DIESEL

R

▲ Keeping the insides of the big diesel engine clean was important. Large filters on the exterior of the power plant handled this chore.

◄ To better navigate water-logged rice and cane fields, the front tires wore heavy-duty ribs that facilitated added directional control.

Above: *For protection from the wet conditions that were part of rice and cane farming, tractor had to be equipped with addition guards to keep the running gear dry.*

Right: *Gears were chosen using this stout lever.*

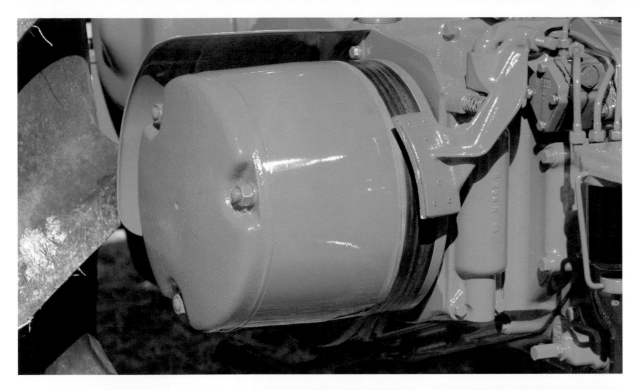

Left: The clutch allowed for smoother motion in forward and reverse gears and provided a power source for belt-driven accessories.

Below: The 1949 Model R was the first diesel-powered John Deere. The efficient engine quickly earned its place in the hearts of farmers who wanted to save money on fuel costs.

The standard tread layout could be ordered in a wheatland style or in this rice field configuration with the front wheels wide apart.

Far Left: Adding a touch of flash to this restored Model R are the chrome-plated "John Deere" badges affixed to the tractor's sheet metal.

Far Bottom Left: Hydraulics that made easier work of attaching required accessories added to the selling features of the John Deere Model R.

Left: To deliver added traction in wet field conditions, the rear tires of tractors equipped for rice and cane farming incorporated heavier lugs.

given extra-protection for toiling in the wet rice paddies and cane fields. The heavy-duty tires were of a more deeply-ribbed design for added traction in the soggy earth. According to its current owner, when this Model R was discovered, it was in terrible condition due to years or working in rice fields and a long period of neglect.

The shipping weight for this bruiser is claimed to be 7,652 pounds. That includes a full compliment of rice-and-cane equipment. The base cost for a 1954 model was $3,650. The rice-and-cane version sold for $4,240. More than 20,000 copies of the Model R were shipped to the US, Canada and overseas during its production span.

That padded seat on this 70 Series diesel looks a lot more comfy than the older metal saddles.

Following in the path left by the Model G, the Model 70 was built between the years of 1953 and 1956. Unlike the G it replaced, the 70 could be had in a choice of standard and row-crop configurations. An LPG-fueled version was produced first, for 1954, and a diesel-powered version was added in 1955. As on many tractors of the day, a distillate or All-Fuel option was a carryover choice for the 70.

This 1956 Model 70 is fitted with the diesel engine and started with a smaller, gas-fired V-4 pony engine. Using the smaller, more-efficient engine to start the rumbling diesel saves time and fuel. Turning over a diesel engine in cold weather is a challenging proposition and the pony engine serves this function. A six-volt battery is used to turn the smaller engine over. (Non-diesel versions of the 70 were fitted and fired by a pair of 12-volt batteries.)

The displacements of each type of engine varied, but all Model 70s were in the 50-hp class. Marvel-Schebler carburetors were used on gasoline and All-Fuel versions of the 70, with John Deere carburetors on the LPG-fueled model. Regardless of the engine used, all Model 70s employed a new intake-valve design. It included a "raised eyebrow" that "disrupted" the fuel as it flowed into the engine and bolstered fuel blending. In diesel-engine versions, additional rigidity was gained by adding a center main bearing.

In all Model 70s, forward motion was controlled by a six-speed gearbox that utilized John Deere's tried-and-true two-stick system carried over from previous models. To try to level the playing field with gas a LPG versions of the 70 in the speed department, the diesel model carried different gear ratios. Forward speeds as high as 12.5 mph were achieved in top gear. A solitary reverse gear was included. It could propel the 70 backwards at 3.25 mph when it was engaged. Considering the 70's heavy weight of more than four tons, both top speeds seemed quite remarkable.

The Model 70 came with standard tread, row-crop or high-crop front axles up front and weighed about the same regardless of the option selected. Overall length was 136 inches and height was 66 inches to the top of the hood. In 1956, the basic, standard-tread model 70 retailed for $2,750 and the diesel was $675 additional. With the diesel- powered 70, a rating of 1,125 rpm was on tap, compared to 975 rpm for tractors with other types of engines. The diesel model's gasoline starting motor was rated at 5,500 rpm, with the higher speed required to crank the big diesel into action. Fuel economy of the 70 diesel was 17.72 horsepower gallons per hour, compared to 11.2 for the gas version, 11.06 for the All-Fuel version and 9.57 for the LP gas engine. This figure was also among the highest recorded in Nebraska Tractor Tests and increased sales of diesels.

The John Deere Model 70 diesel
delivered fuel economy of 17.72 hp
hours per gallon.

JOHN DEERE   *DIESEL*

70

Power Steer

▲ John Deere's Roll-O-Matic option greatly increased the Model 70 tractor's flexibility of use and allowed it to do more jobs around a farm.

◀ Comfort is a big part of field work and the well-padded pillion seat of the Model 70 made for a moderately "comfy" perch.

Weighing over 7,000 pounds, the Model 70 diesel was a hefty load.

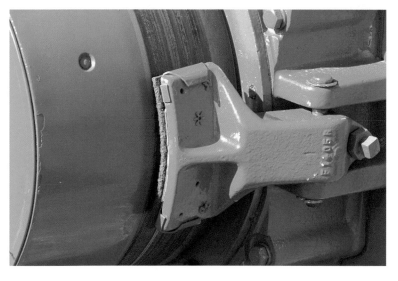

Top Left: *While the diesel engine of the Model 70 Diesel did the heavy work, a smaller, gasoline-fed pony engine got things going.*

Above: *Rated at 50.4 maximum belt horsepower in Nebraska Tractor Test No, 598, the diesel version of the model 70 provided all the power required to run needed accessories.*

Right: *The cast rear wheels on this Model 70 carry 13x 38-inch tires. Other sizes were also available to meet the needs of different types of farming operations.*

Above: *Connections for hydraulic accoutrements could be easily made by attaching to any one of the outlets found on the rear of the Model 70 tractor.*

Right: *When compared to some of Deere's earlier models, the instrument panel on the Model 70 had a fairly complete layout of gauges and controls.*

Production of the Model 70 was quartered at Deere's Waterloo, Iowa plant and more than 41,000 copies were turned out during its three-year assembly period. The example pictured here is equipped with Deere's Roll-O-Matic front axle, a popular choice of buyers. The owner of this tractor grew up around Model 50 and 60 units and used to think the 70 was the largest tractor in the world. He finds the ancillary starting motor a unique feature of this fabulous farming machine.

This well-outfitted 195g John Deere Model 70 is equipped with power steering.

1957 620

Front radiator badge featured the leaping-deer in green on a yellow background.

Tractor sales are very new-product driven. History shows that leaving the same tractor on the sales floor too long can hurt sales. Doing this makes it appear as if the tractor maker is resting on its laurels, while the competition is moving ahead. Although John Deere was planning completely-revamped New-Generation models for 1960, it did not want to lose any transitional buyers during the development period. So Deere designers sharpened their pencils and hit the drawing boards.

A Twenty Series was created to fill the gap between the current models and the New-Generation Thirty Series. Knowing full well that the 620 was to be a temporary model, Deere was not about to start a total redesign from scratch. Instead, the company used a lot of the donor Model 60's technology to get the 620 project moving.

Cosmetically, the 620 looked like a yellow-striped version of the Model 60 it was replacing, but further evidence of change was easily unearthed. Under the hood of the 620 was a reduced-displacement 303-cubic-inch two-cylinder engine. Although this engine was 18 cubic inches smaller than the Model 60 engine, it was fitted with aluminum pistons and revised combustion chambers that resulted in a power increase. Its operating rpm was also increased from the 975rpm the Model 60 produced to 1,125 rpm. To ensure that the newfound power wasn't wasted, the final-drive, PTO and clutch components were enhanced. Additional ballasting in the front of a strengthened frame also provided better balance and more durability.

With increased power, tractors typically lose some fuel efficiency, but this wasn't the case where the 620 was concerned. The more powerful engine was actually more of a "fuel sipper" and this, combined with a fuel tank that was two gallons larger, put longer stints in the field within the farmer's grasp.

First seen in 1957, the John Deere 620 carried the green-faced dashboard of the Model 60, but it did wear distinctive yellow accents on the sides of the hood and cowl.

As with nearly every model John Deere produced then, the 620 could be equipped with a variety of front-axle options. Choices included everything from a single front wheel to extra-long axles that put 120 inches between the wheels. The dual-tricycle format was still probably most prevalent, because of its "do-everything" characteristics. Measuring 135 inches in length and clocking in at more than 8,500 pounds when ready for battle, the John Deere 620 was neither the largest nor the smallest tractor on the market in its day.

Fluctuations in sales and the fickle nature of the customer base dictated that the 620 be replaced only two years after it was introduced. Therefore, 1957 and 1958 were the only years this Model 60 replacement tractor was available. The Model 630 followed close on the heels of the 620 and helped fill the "blank space" left between previous offerings and the upcoming New-Generation models.

Lettering identified the manufacturer, model designation and power steering option.

▲ Smaller in displacement than the Model 60's two-cylinder engine, the 303-cid twin used in the Model 620 delivered more power because it of design improvements that made it more efficient.

◄ 44.25 belt horsepower was available to drive accessories connected to the spinning drum that also served as the John Deere 620 tractor's clutch.

Above: *Of the many options John Deere offered, the dual tricycle wheels were probably the one most often seen rolling across the plains.*

Top Right: *This huge flywheel was "in charge" of keeping the 620's engine running smoothly and it provided balance and smooth operation no matter what the load.*

Right: *Hoping to absorb at least some of the bumps encountered during typical field work, this hydraulic shock absorber was installed on the Model 620 to squelch some of the tractor's bouncing motions.*

Far Left: *As did other John Deere models, the 620 featured a large-diameter steering wheel that made it easier to "muscle" the tractor around the terrain on a farm.*

Left: *The extended axles of the 620 allowed farmers to adjust the width of the drive wheels to suit different planting and harvesting requirements.*

Vital statistics for 620s included a 135-inch length and a weight over 8,500 pounds.

1958 620

Many chassis components had to be beefed up to handle the 620's added power.

As a young man, Tom Schroeder first worked farm fields with a John Deere 620. Not only was he exposed to this tractor in his formative years, but it was a model that was sold in the year he was born. Thus, he decided he had to purchase one and that is what set his tractor-collecting passion into motion. Tom jumped at the opportunity to own this particular 620 when it once crossed an auction block. It was fully restored by local craftsmen.

The 620 was first sold in 1957. It was a more powerful tractor than the Model 60 that it replaced. John Deere's target for the 620 was a 20 percent boost in output over other 600 series tractors. So, that's what the 620 model name was supposed to represent. Total production of the 620 was 22,532 units over a four-year period. The standard version was built through 1958 and the orchard model was continued through 1960.

The 620 employed a 302.9-cid two-cylinder engine that was of typical John Deere design. The gasoline-fired models relied on a 6.2:1 compression ratio. The engine was rated at 1,125 rpm. As mentioned in the previous chapter, the 620 actually used a smaller-displacement engine than the 60, but it had lighter-weight aluminum pistons and better combustion characteristics that added to its ability to churn out power. Many of the reciprocating parts were also improved and these, too, contributed to better performance and fuel economy.

Several variations of the 620 were sold, including high-crop, orchard and standard-tread models. Gasoline, LPG and All-Fuel versions of the 302.9-cid engine were offered as well. The different fuel systems had an affect on both power output and fuel economy, but the size of the engine was the same for all three.

The power was sent through a gearbox that offered six forward speeds and a single reverse gear. A top forward speed of 11.5 mph was achievable in sixth gear. Weighing just under 3 tons, the gas-fired 620 carried 22.25 gallons of fuel and returned a rating of 12.5 hours of work per gallon of fuel.

Many chassis components on the Model 620 tractor had to be beefed up above Model 60 specifications to handle the 620's added power. They included the PTO, the gears, the clutch and the final-drive system. The front portion of the frame was also bolstered and ballasted for added stability. Total fuel tank capacity was raised to allow two additional gallons to be carried.

The narrow front end fitted to this example also includes the "Roll-O-Matic" power-steering system that John Deere invented. When equipped as a high-crop tractor, the axle width was adjustable, but all of the tractors carried fixed tread spacing of 55.5 inches. Overall length of the 620 was 135 inches with a height of 66 inches. Adjustment to the rear axle was achieved by using a rack-and-pinion quick-change system.

This 1958 John Deere 620 diesel was built at the company's Waterloo Tractor Works.

▲ *The clutch mechanism could do double-duty as a belt drive, but this tractor's fresh-looking paint tells us that it has yet to see "time in the trenches" since being restored.*

◄ *Added comfort was gained by adding an optional Float-Ride seat to your John Deere tractor.*

Above: *As often seen on heavy-duty tractors, a massive flywheel located behind this housing keeps the power flowing smoothly.*

Right: *A larger steering wheel reduced the effort required to steer the John Deere Model 620.*

There's no job in the world like photographing a beautifully-restored tractor on a beautiful sunny afternoon!

Above: Strong vertical lines characterized the front grille of the 620, which carried a large John Deere badge.

Top Right: A dual tricycle arrangement was found on standard row-crop versions of the Model 620, which had 6.00 x 16 tires installed on the tractors steel rims.

Right: John Deere's "Roll-O-Matic" power steering made the task of turning the 620 easier.

Numerous options were available for 620 models. This tractor, which was built at John Deere's Waterloo Tractor Works, in Waterloo, Iowa, carries several of them. It is a so-called "black dash" model – made only in 1958 and nicknamed after the dark-painted hue of the dashboard. These tractors could be ordered with a cigarette lighter and fuel gauge, both of which this example carries. The new "Float-Ride" seat brought new levels of comfort to tractor users. Steel clamshell fenders were another option, as was the tractor's three-point hitch.

Other changes the 620 had from Model 60 specifications included a larger steering wheel, sealed-beam headlights and a more-efficient muffler that improved the exhaust system. Retail pricing for the 1958 Model 620 row-crop tractor was set at $2,650 before any options were added.

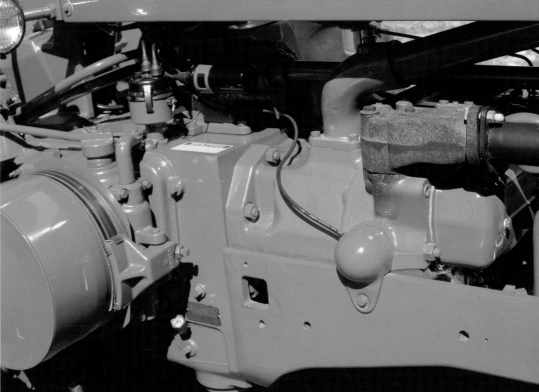

Above: Displacing 302.9 cubic inches, the smaller two-cylinder engine in the 620 produced more power than the engine used in the Model 60 that it replaced.

Top Right: The 620 model number and a "Power Steering" call-out were included in the graphics applied to the cowl.

1958 720

Dry shipping weight for the dual-front-wheel 720 was 6,790 pounds.

The 1958 John Deere 720 seen here led a full and productive life on a farm for almost four decades. It was used to work an 80-acre parcel with a set of four 14-inch plow bottoms in tow. Upon his retirement from active farming, the tractor's previous owner approached Stan and Diane Rakers about buying the unit. The parties reached agreement and a refurbishment began. The retired farmer wanted to be updated as the 720 was restored. Sadly, he passed away only months before the restoration was completed.

The 720 was another evolutionary unit from John Deere. It was introduced as a 1957 model. Seeing no need to re-invent the wheel, the manufacturer simply found ways to improve and upgrade previous models.

Following in the tracks of the 70, the 720 featured an all-new gas-powered engine. The revised power plant had a higher 1,125-rpm operating speed and a 20 percent gain in horsepower. A raft of small changes produced the added power, while a dipstick for checking the oil level seemed like a minor, but welcome improvement.

Diesel versions of the 720 used a 376-cid two-cylinder horizontal engine had the same design and displacement as the Model 70's diesel. There were internal alterations to the pistons, intake valves and injectors that added 10 hp. The 70 had set industry standards for fuel economy for three decades, but the more powerful 720

was nearly as economical to operate. In Nebraska Tractor Test No. 594, it posted 16.56 horsepower hours per gallon of fuel.

Shifting gears on the 720 was improved. A single-lever mechanism replaced the two-lever unit of the 70. Alterations to the gear ratios gave the 720 a true low speed "creeper" gear and 1958 models could be fitted with optional gearing that allowed for a top speed of 11.5 mph. The single reverse gear allowed a speed up to about 3 mph.

To compliment the added power and speed, the brakes on the 720 were also enhanced, as was its power steering. John Deere's Custom Powr-Trol included revised "Load-and-Depth Control and was joined by a three-point hitch. Remote cylinders for the hydraulics could also be added, This permitted equipment to be disconnected with no loss of fluid. For 720s with manual steering, the pedestals were weighted to equal the weight of the power steering models. This change provided the same feel and balance, regardless of the steering system ordered.

The foot pedal for the PTO now featured three distinct positions, for better control. No longer was the non-live version of the PTO offered.

Further fine tuning was applied to 1958 models, including John Deere's black-faced dashboard. Although nothing more than a cosmetic upgrade, the "black-dash" 720s are considered a great find by modern-day collectors. To provide a decorative, yet frugal,

Looking right at home of the farm, the John Deere 720 was a very adaptable tractor.

▲ When the clutch was engaged, the farmer could easily drive his 720 in either direction.

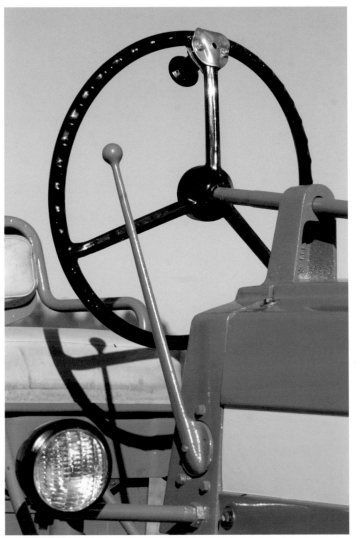

◀ Whether connected to the optional power steering or the "old-school" manual steering, the large-diameter steering wheel was "on duty" to control the direction of a 720.

Above: Typical styling for the nose of the 720 included sturdy vertical bars that concealed the radiator behind them.

Top Right: Upgrades in the comfort department could be ordered by selecting the optional "Float-Ride Seat" when buying a John Deere 720.

Right: 15.5-38 six-ply rear tires could be chosen for the John Deere 720 over the standard 13.6-38 rear tires.

graphics treatment, the yellow stripe and panels on the 720 was a large decal, instead of the painted trim used previously. The decal looked great, but saved time by eliminating the need to mask and paint each tractor built.

A long list of options could be ordered for 720 models, making each tractor that John Deere delivered an individualized machine. Available options included a speed-hour gauge and a cigarette lighter, An electric fuel gauge was standard on 720 diesels. A Float Ride seat with a foam rubber pad made for a more comfortable farming experience.

Shipping weight for the dual-front-wheel 720 (without fluids or fuel) was 6,790 pounds. The gasoline version had a 26-1/2 gallon fuel tank. A 10-quart crankcase was bolted on the 360.5-cid engine. 🦌

Above: Available in diesel, gasoline, LPG and all-fuel configurations, the 720 engines were true workhorses. The gas job was more powerful than the unit used in the Model 70 that the 720 replaced.

Left: The yellow accent panels on the John Deere 720 were applied as a large decal, rather than by painting, as had been the case previously.

1959 330

*A dry shipping weight of the 720
was 2,600 pounds and made it
easy to handle.*

Since the formation of the company, the John Deere legacy had been formed around the use of two-cylinder engines. Seeing a trend towards larger and more powerful machinery, Deere laid the groundwork for a New-Generation of tractors with three-, four- and six-cylinder engines.

Deere's original agenda had the Twenty Series being supplanted with the freshly- minted New-Generation models, but a minor delay forced the company to design a stop gap model to ensure continued sales until the new tractors were ready.

The Twenty Series was revamped and became the Thirty Series. Largely the same as the tractors they replaced, the Thirties were still upgraded with some important features that to draw new buyers into showrooms. Styling issues were addressed by the now famous staff at Henry Dreyfuss Associates. Smoother sheet metal contours lent an air of newness to the mostly-unchanged 330. Revisions to the tractor included a dashboard with a more rakish angle and a more comfortable steering wheel.

One challenge in selling a small tractor is keeping the cost of ownership on par with the diminished capabilities of the unit being sold. With the 330 being a fairly small model, the price tag had to be kept in line. Deere didn't want to force people to turn to another brand to get a product in their price range. One way to control price was to reduce the number configurations the 330 came in to less than what was offered on most of Deere's other tractors.

The 330 was limited to two primary designs: the 330U and the 330S. These were the utility and standard models. Having just two kept production variations to a minimum and held down manufacturing costs. A handful of 330V "Southern Specials" were also built, but the 330U with 247 assemblies and the 330S with 844 assemblies accounted for most of the sales.

Another cost-cutting measure involved eliminating the all-fuel option. For the last two years of 330 production, all tractors built – regardless of model -- had gasoline-engines. A 100.5-cid two-cylinder horizontal engine was used in the 330.

When fitted with the 9.00 x 24 rear tires and wheels, the four-speed gearbox could propel the 330 to a top speed of 12 mph. Only one reverse gear was provided, limiting the backward motion to 1.62 mph. With 1,650 rpm measured at the PTO, the diminutive 330 was capable of driving some good-sized ancillary equipment. Tipping the scales at around 2,600 pounds, the 330 was easy to move around the farm, regardless of the type of terrain.

Of the "tweaks" applied to the 330 models, one major alteration was a new oil filter location. It was moved from the valve cover to the engine block. At that location, the oil filler was joined by a dipstick, which could be used to check the oil level. One feature taken away from the 330U was hydraulics.

One change in 330 models was a new oil filter location as seen in this profile view.

▲ Capable of pulling some fairly heavy equipment, the 330 was often fitted with front-end counterweights to compensate for the weight of the implement being towed.

◀ Outstanding features of the John Deere 330 included the steeply-angled steering wheel that aided directional control and the black-faced dash that increased gauge visibility.

Above: The narrow face of the John Deere 330 was proportionate to the rest of its compact size. It carried a prominent Deere logo and "330" identification.

Top Right: The padded seat could be upgraded to Deere's Float-Ride system when a buyer indicated that he wanted that option on the order sheet.

Right: A three-point hitch had become almost standard in the tractor industry. Despite its small size, the John Deere 330 came equipped with one and was ready to pull it.

Prospective buyers said they had no need for hydraulics and felt like they would rather not pay for an item they couldn't use.

The last 330 rolled out of the John Deere Tractor Works in Waterloo, Iowa in February 1960. The Thirty Series had done an admirable job of filling the gap between the Twenties and New-Generation models. The short 2-year life cycle of these tractors makes any sighting of them an uncommon experience today. 🦌

With its sturdy PTO the little 330 was could drive some big accessories.

1959 430

This tractor pulls a Deere 246/247 corn planter that could seed two rows at once.

With its lineage reaching all the way back to the Model M, the John Deere 430 had a strong bloodline backing it up. The 430 was not a revolutionary model. It was part of the transitional Thirty Series released to satisfy the new-product demands of buyers until all-new three-, four- and six-cylinder tractors arrived. There were few differences between the 430 and the 420 it replaced, but small steps were taken to improve the 430.

The 113.3-cid horizontal two-cylinder engine was carried over for the 430. It developed 27 hp at the drawbar. No belt drive was factory-fitted to the 430. When one was purchased and installed, 29 hp were measured at the spinning cylinder. A 1,850-rpm rating for the PTO provided ample rotation when a powered implement was pulled behind the 430.

The tractor's design carried on the tradition of using the engine and gearbox as stressed members, thereby eliminating the need for a true chassis. This construction kept weight and costs down, thus allowing the 430 to appeal to a wider audience. The question of the frameless design never worked against the 430, which proved to be one of Deere's most accepted models.

Part of the interest in the 430 stemmed from the wide variety of axle setups that could be ordered for it. Tricycle, row-crop, high-crop and even crawler options were seen on the order sheet, making this a tractor for nearly every purpose. Fuel options were also numerous with gasoline, All-Fuel and LPG versions of the 430 being offered, along with a 435 diesel. Transmissions options for the 430 included gearboxes with four or five forward speeds.

Taking the place of a standard reverse gear, a directional "reverser" was installed and allowed the operator to use any of the forward gears to go in the opposite direction.

Upping the bar when compared to some of Deere's larger models, the 430 featured the easier-to-read slanted dashboard and a steering wheel that came to rest in a "friendlier" location. Joining these features was an improved pillion with a more deeply-cushioned seat for added comfort.

When it came to features that made the 430 more desirable in the field, the three-point hitch, hydraulic outlets and optional remote cylinder for power steering scored high in the rankings. The three-point hitch was also given load-and-depth control for more confident cultivation. Perhaps the ultimate in big tractor features added to the 430 was the available power-adjusted rear wheels.

In the style department, there weren't too many changes from the 420 to the 430. The font of the "John Deere" logo was unchanged, but the "430" model identification was now applied in a shadowed text.

Rated to pull a two- or three-bottom plow, this 1959 model has been accessorized with a Deere 246/247 corn planter. When pulled behind the 430, this planter could seed two rows at once. The steel wheels tracked neatly behind the donor power supply -- the 430 itself! Other options for this tractor included an eight-foot disc that worked well if the soil was not overly stubborn.

The 430 was listed for only two years, 1959 and 1960. After that, Deere released an all-new line of bigger-and-better tractors.

Of the many tasks the John Deere 430 was capable of performing, playing host to a spreader was the most common.

▲ *All four hoppers could be filled with seed corn so that a good bit of acreage could be covered before stopping to refill them.*

◄ *New on the 430 were positive features like the slanted face of the instrument panel, the revised angle of the steering wheel and an ergonomically-improved seat.*

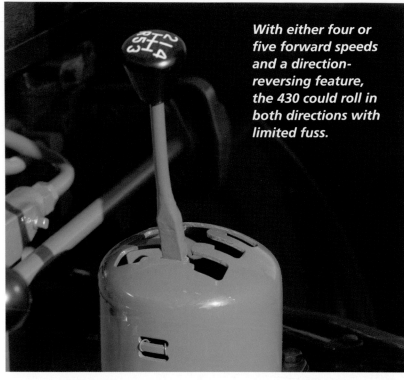

With either four or five forward speeds and a direction-reversing feature, the 430 could roll in both directions with limited fuss.

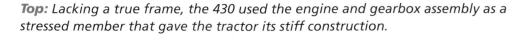

Top: Lacking a true frame, the 430 used the engine and gearbox assembly as a stressed member that gave the tractor its stiff construction.

Above: The John Deere Model 246/247 corn planter was easy to identify because of the large numbers emblazoned on its rails.

Right: The angled faces of the steel wheels provided sure footing in the roughest soil conditions and helped the 430 track straight.

These wheels were chain-driven to ensure confident rotation and even distribution of the seed.

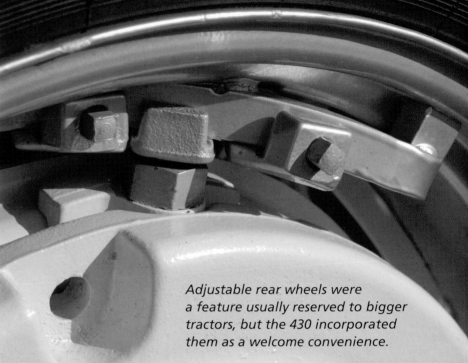

Adjustable rear wheels were a feature usually reserved to bigger tractors, but the 430 incorporated them as a welcome convenience.

The planter's steel wheels track neatly behind this John Deere 430 tractor.

A new steering wheel that angled up to the farmer improved the 630's comfort level.

As mentioned in the two previous chapters, the John Deere Thirty was simply an updated Twenty that gave dealers something different to sell until the New-Generation tractors arrived. Both the Twenty and Thirty models were considered direct descendents of the 1934 Model A, which earned the John Deere Tractor Company a solid reputation for dependability.

Tractors in the 1959 Thirty Series bore a striking resemblance to the machines they replaced, though they had improvements and extras to further enhance the breed. The reliable power trains and running gear used had already forged a place in the history books, so little was done to alter their designs. One change was the installation of an elliptical "Oval-Tone" exhaust muffler that protruded through the hood. Previous mufflers were of a more basic, tubular design. The new oval contour helped quiet the departing fumes.

Very subtle changes were seen in the 630's sheet metal, which was generally more curvaceous. But, there were no major changes to the design, as Deere felt the money would be better spent on development of the following all-new models.

A facet of the 630 that was addressed was ergonomics. Taking the place of the nearly vertical steering wheel of the 620 was one that was angled upward for improved comfort. The face of the dashboard was also tilted to mimic the angle of the steering wheel. A farmer could also order Deere's vastly-improved Float-Ride seat — a pleasanter perch for long days in the field. A new push-button starter simplified cranking the engine to life.

Steel clamshell fenders were a popular option for the 630. They protected the operator from flying debris and made it easier to get into the seat by grasping the contoured shape of a fender when climbing aboard. A set of four headlights could also be added to allow use of the 630 after the sun had fallen beyond the horizon.

The 630 was still powered by the same 302.9-cid engine that the 620 used. It was available in gasoline, All-Fuel and LPG versions. Six forward gear ratios were at hand and the 630 could reach speeds up to 11.5 mph. The single reverse gear provided a speed of only 3 mph but was adequate for the limited time a tractor needed to be operated in that direction. There were many configurations for the 630 including row-crop, high-crop and single-front-wheel options. A rating of 44 belt hp was listed for the gasoline version of the 630, with 1,125 rpm at the PTO.

The 630 was only sold in 1959 and 1960 to bridge the gap between the 620 and the soon-to-be released New-Generation tractors. Although little changed, it fulfilled a needed role and gave Deere the breathing room it needed to bring fresh machines to market.

Subtle changes in the 630's sheet metal gave it a more curvaceous appearance.

A rating of 44 belt hp – not applicable to this particular tractor which has no belt drive -- was listed for the gasoline version of the 630, with 1,125 rpm at the PTO.

An optional Float-Ride seat provided operators with new levels of comfort.

Above: *The "mellow-tone" muffler used on the 630 was of an oval shape and helped to quiet the noise caused by backpressure from the departing fumes.*

Top Right: *The high-crop version of the 630 set the front wheels high and wide, leaving plenty of clearance for working tall crops.*

Right: *A balanced flywheel kept the engine running smoothly.*

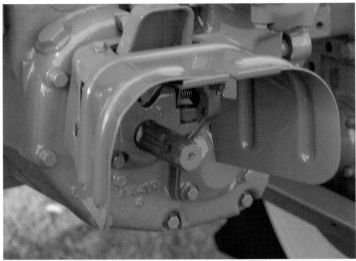

Far Left: Powr-Trol hydraulics were installed to deliver smooth operation from those implements requiring pressurized controls.

Left: Shielded for protection, the PTO shaft delivered plenty of torque to the implements that required power.

The 302.9-cid two-cylinder horizontal engine of the 630 was mated to a six-speed gearbox. This was the same reliable engine the 620 had used.

1959 730

The 730 quickly became one of John Deere's most popular tractors.

Though it was based on the earlier 720 model, the 730 would go on to become one of John Deere's most popular machines on its own. Its production even continued overseas once assembly operations in Waterloo, Iowa had ceased.

The owner of this beautiful tractor, collector Dustin Schroeder, was hoisted into the saddle of a 730 back when he was a child. He always remembered that experience, but it wasn't until 2005 that Schroeder finally located a 730 that satisfied his desire to own one. Then, he added this big John Deere to his outstanding collection.

Though based on the tried-and-true 720, the new 730 took more time than expected to go through research and development. The roll-out wouldn't be complete until 1960. Then, the John Deere 730 quickly earned a place as one of the company's most popular tractors. The combination of appearance revisions, operating economy and a strong power train made the tractor, which was built at the Waterloo Works, a winner.

The new tractor offered a variety of engines and fuel options. This example carries the 375.6-cid diesel engine in its stout frame. This power plant was rated at the same 1,125 rpm as gasoline models, but of course needed a much higher 16.0:1 compression ratio. As usual with a diesel, a small gasoline-fed V-4 pony engine was an integral part of the diesel package. It allowed the owner to get the sometimes hard-to-start, two-cylinder diesel fired up.

Diesel models also carried a six-volt battery, rather than the 12-volt type used in other models.

Gasoline, LPG and All-Fuel engines – all 360.5-cid -- could also be had in a 730. The gasoline and All-Fuel engines used Marvel-Schebler carburetors (Model DLTX-95 with gas and DLTX-98 with All-Fuel), while the LPG version used a John Deere AF2828R to mete out the needed gas. A 20-gallon receptacle stored fuel, except on the LPG-optioned tractors.

If buyers saw a chink in the 730's armor, it was that the transmission was still of six-speeds-forward/one-speed-reverse design. Deere had hoped the expansive torque curve of the engine would compensate for the lack of added gearing, but some farmers wished for a few more gear ratios. This did little to hurt the popularity of the big 730, which went on to gain great acceptance.

As usual, the chassis of the John Deere tractor could be configured to meet a farmer's needs. The row-crop layout could be found with one or two front wheels in dual-tricycle, fixed or wide-front configurations. The high-crop variant had a pair of wide-spaced tires, mounted up high, so the tractor could clear tall crops. The 730 was 136 long and 66 inches high. Depending on the type of power plant, weights ranged from 6,183 pounds for the LPG version with dual-tricycle tires up to 6,533 pounds for the diesel with its auxiliary engine. In addition to adding pounds, the diesel option added $750 to the tractor's price.

1959 730

The use of an oval muffler was
continued on the 730's exhaust stack.

JOHN DEERE

730

DIESEL

Power Steering

▲ Capable of providing 58.84 belt hp, the diesel model was the most powerful version of the 730.

◄ A dual-tricycle front wheel arrangement was one of several configurations that could be ordered for a 730.

Above: In front of the 730 was a massive front grille carrying the John Deere logo.

Right: This tractor carries the 375.6-cid diesel engine and has a call-out to prove it.

Above: *This rack-and-pinion gear could be employed to adjust the rear track width of a 730.*

Top Right: *The center hub extended beyond the face of the steel wheel to facilitate rear-track adjustments.*

Right: *The twin stacks handled incoming and exiting fumes.*

On Dustin Schroeder's 730, the dual-tricycle tires are accompanied by Deere's Roll-O-Matic power steering. The tractor also uses reversible disc wheels. The rear tread can be altered using the rack-and-pinion type quick-change system. A set of Deluxe fenders are also in place on this 1959 model, which carries a three-point hitch mounted below the chassis. The optional Float-Ride provides the operator with a comfy perch. Starting this 730 is accomplished with the help of the optional electric-starting system.

Production numbers for the 730 totaled 29,713tractors and 16,212 of those carried the electric start option. After production of this model closed in Iowa, the tooling and parts were shipped to a plant in Rosario, Argentina and assembly of 730s went on there until 1968. Every tractor built in Argentina had the electric-start kit and high-crop, row-crop and standard models were constructed. Additional production of the 730 occurred in Monterey, Mexico and it involved mainly high-crop diesel-powered tractors.

This John Deere 730 is powered by a two-cylinder diesel engine. A gas-fired V-4 pony engine is provided to help get the diesel started.

This row-crop utility tractor carries headlights to allow night use after dark.

While the true nature of a tractor is a machine for field duty, some "lucky" units get a second life after farming. This 1960 John Deere 435 Diesel became a show tractor. Local shows feature tractor performance contests and "tractor pulling" is such an event. In such venues, a weighted "sled" is attached to modified tractors and the machine that pulls it furthest wins. A device that increases the sled's friction the farther it is dragged makes things more entertaining.

The 435 we see here has been altered for tractor pulls. Hung between its front wheels is extra weight that compensates for the load being pulled. The front wheels are also of a smaller diameter than those used to work in fields. The tractor's pulling power was also enhanced by installing larger fuel injectors on its two-cylinder motor. The stock 10.5-gallon fuel tank did not have to be changed, however, since the tractor makes only short runs in the pulling events.

Obviously the 435 wasn't factory-designed for tractor pulls. Its real purpose was to provide the operator with a tractor that had product differences from its predecessor, the 430. Where the 430 was available with three fuel-system options, the 435 came only as a diesel model. The two-cylinder General Motors diesel fit perfectly into the 435 and delivered the combination of increased efficiency and power that diesels are known for.

In the GM design, incoming oxygen flowed through ports in the cylinder walls and only exhaust valves were needed. A Roots-type blower added some boost to the incoming blend. The relatively small 106.2-cid diesel delivered a lot of power for its size. The engine was coupled to a transmission with five forward speeds and a single reverse gear. To make the best use of engine power, the gear ratios were picked to provide good speed.

To simplify manufacturing, the 435 came only as a row-crop style utility tractor, which was historically John Deere's most popular format for this type of tractor. A long list of optional gear was still available. These included different-size wheels and tires, weights for the rear drive wheels, a 1,000-rpm PTO, remote hydraulics and a low-slung exhaust. Later models could have power steering, as well.

The 435 was built in 1959 and sold as a 1960 model with 4,625 units being assembled each, The spec-sheet shipping weight was 4,100 pounds. The base price was $3,190, but the lengthy list of options could easily drive that number higher.

This 1960 John Deere 435 Diesel owned by Santa-Deere Farms is a show tractor.

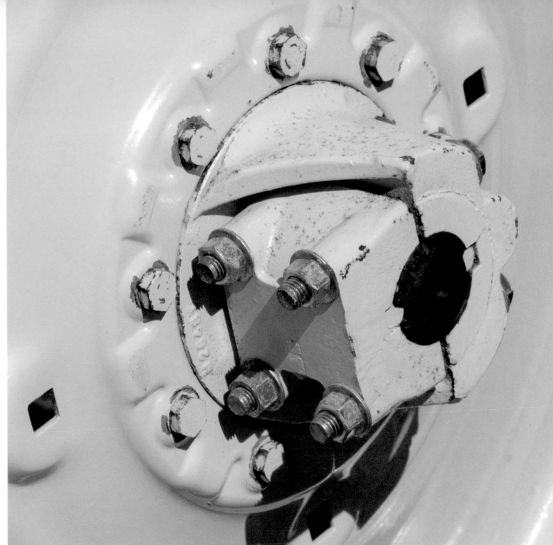

▲ A sturdy rear wheel hub was used on the John Deere 435.

◀ Another feature added for use in tractor pulls was small-diameter front tires and wheels.

Above: The radiator grille of the 435 was squared off and masculine looking.

Top Right: This 435 has been modified for tractor pulls and carries an additional block of weight on the front axle.

Right: There was no mistaking the fact that GM made the diesel engine used in the John Deere 435 tractor.

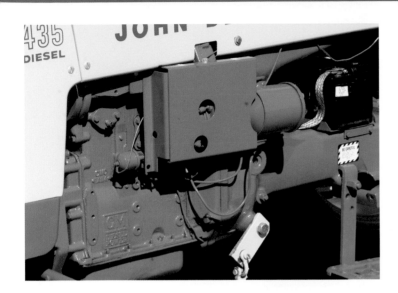

Far Left: *By installing a GM motor into the frame of the 435, John Deere saved time and money.*

Left: *The Float-Ride seat was a popular option with John Deere customers.*

The powerful-for-its-size 106.2-cid diesel is fitted with a Rootes-type blower.

Competition among tractor builders remained strong in the late-1950s. Even the mighty John Deere was forced to be more creative to sell its farming machines. As we've seen earlier, instead of crafting an all-new tractor, the Twenty Series was dressed up in some new "duds" for 1959 and rolled out as the Thirty Series.

Henry Dreyfuss and Associates was again tapped as the creative force to make the styling changes. As a first step, the industrial designers smoothed out the masculine lines and harsh edges of the Twenty Series models. This evolutionary revision brought a new profile to the series, without causing trouble. A set of flat-topped fenders were added as an option for the 530 model shown here.

These newly-styled fenders featured integrated headlights that improved the tractor's looks and made night use possible. Sturdy handgrips were another part of the design and made the 530 easier to climb into. Dreyfuss was focused on ease and comfort of operation, so small details like these were often seen. A slanted dashboard and an angled steering wheel were two additional tweaks to the 530 design and, while small, these changes added even more to operational convenience.

Beneath the revised sheet metal, the 530 was largely the same as the 520 it replaced. A few minor problems that had been noted on the 520 were addressed in the design of the 530. These included making two versions of the Roll-O-Matic front end available and offering the choice of two wheel sizes for tractors with a single-front-tire arrangement.

A 190-cid two-cylinder engine was carried over from the 520. A diesel was not included on the options list, but LPG, gasoline or All-Fuel choices were. Six forward speeds that could take the 530 to 10 mph and a single reverse gear were found in the gearbox. Depending on the configuration selected, the 530 weighed close to four tons when prepped for duty.

Built for only two years, the 530 had a short life in the John Deere sales catalog. However, it became an important short-run model, as it was largely an extension of the 520.

The serial number on this gasoline-powered row-crop model puts it within 30 tractors from the end of 530 production. Its original destination was the state of Tennessee, which is where it remains today. It was purchased by the current owner in 2002 and restored to perfection in 2003. Since being restored, it has seen active duty in local events, as well as shows in several states.

Left: With dual headlights on this 1960 Deere 530 could keep working after sunset.

A graphic on the side, below the 530 call-out, indicates this tractor has power steering.

Above: The slanted dash and angled steering wheel are both part of the redesign of the Twenty Series that turned it into the Thirty Series.

Top Right: This rear view photo gives a good idea of how fenders protected farmers from debris.

Right: With a rating of 1,325 rpm, the PTO shaft on the rear of the 530 can bring new levels of energy to added implements.

Above: *One of the lower legs of the three-point hitch can be seen here, along with the heavy-duty axle of the drive system.*

Top Right: *Longer spindles and an adjustable width characterize this row-crop version of the 530.*

Right: *The 530's revised steel fenders have a square profile and contain a pair of headlights for improved visibility at night.*

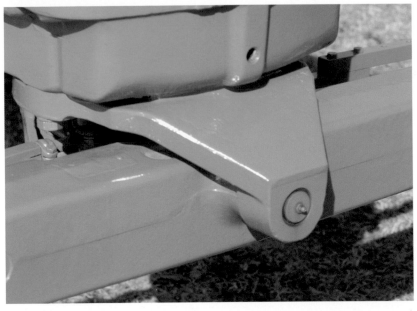

Far Left: Every facet of the 530's construction is designed for heavy-duty use, a fact reflected in this cast-in-steel front-axle pivot.

Left: Having seen duty putting the 38.58 belt hp to good use, the paint on the clutch and belt drive is well worn.

The "John Deere" name even appears on the rear of the tractor's seat.

The 630 was another of John Deere's transitional models designed to fill the gap between the Twenty Series and the soon-to-be-released New-Generation models. To disguise research being done on the upcoming machines, the Thirty Series was developed. It was fairly common knowledge that Deere was working on new tractors, but until the day they arrived, a bit of subterfuge was needed.

Deere wanted to continue using the running gear and power supply of the Twenty Series, while dressing up its shape and making a few modifications. John Deere had a long running relationship with the industrial design firm Henry Dreyfuss and Associates, which was given the nod to refresh the Twenty Series models.

As an update, there was only so much that could be done. Minor alterations in the contours of the sheet metal were made, along with the square fenders being added over the rear wheels.

Rounded fenders were even used on some units, but most had the revised tire covers. A quadrant of headlights was also added to improve visibility at night.

Previous tractors had vertical steering wheels, but now a more natural position was adopted to increase user comfort. Matching that was a slanted dash that also carried a speed-hour gauge.

The 302.9-cid two-cylinder motor from the Twenty Series model was carried over. Its 1,125-rpm PTO shaft rating placed the 630 among the top tractors of the day. It delivered 50.34 hp at the belt as well. Gas, All-Fuel and LPG variations were offered. The latter was the rarest. Fewer than 1,900 were delivered in 1959 and 1960. A top speed of 11.5 mph was possible in sixth gear.

In dual-tricycle-wheel form, the 135-inch-long 630 claimed a weight of nearly 6,000 pounds. A short two-year production run made the 630 a fairly scarce model, but its abilities and improved ergonomics made it a well-received farm machine.

Left: This 630 is set up for lots of accessories to do different jobs right into the dark.

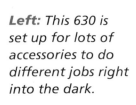

1960 630

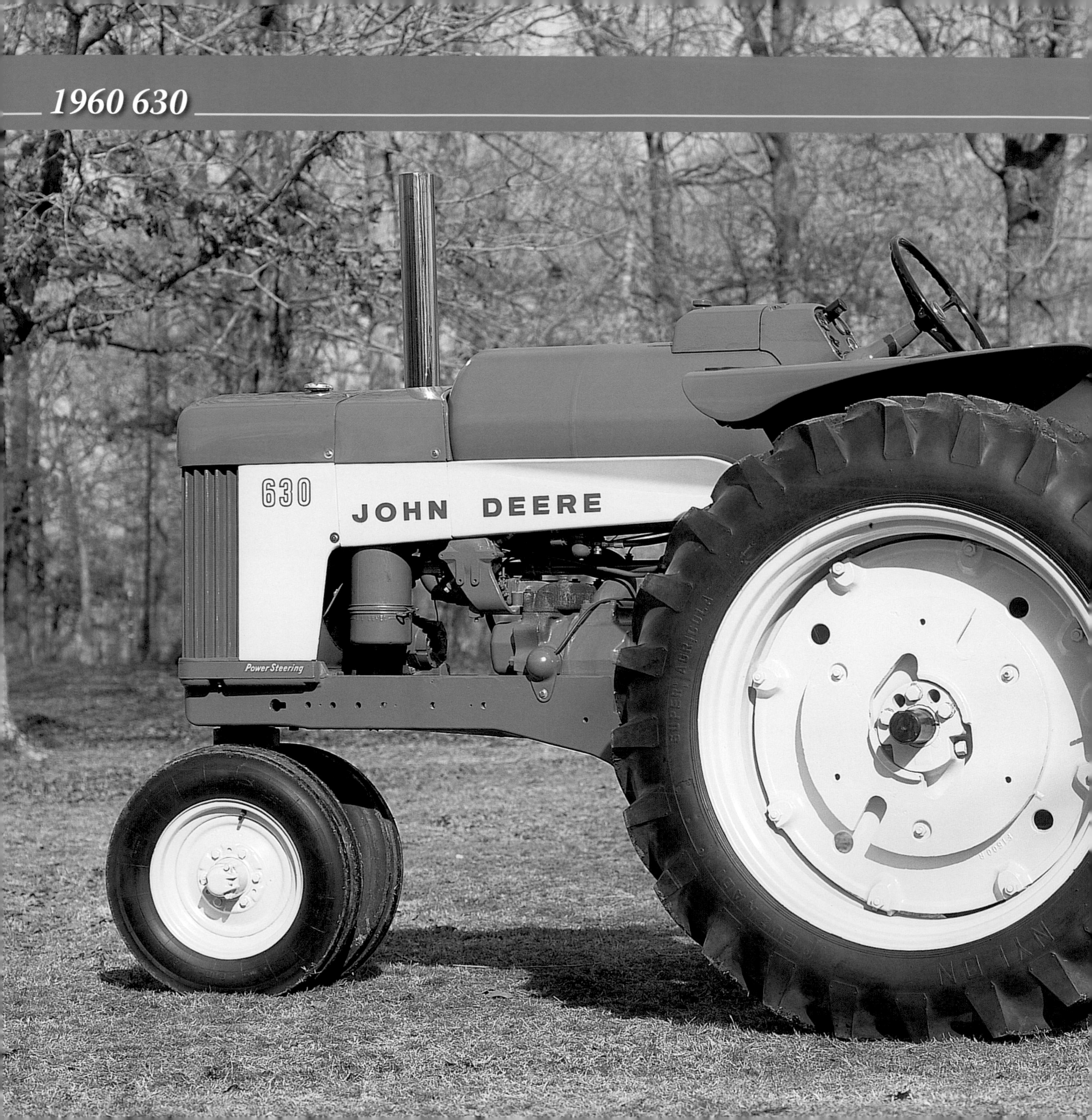
630
JOHN DEERE
Power Steering
SUPER AGRICOLA
NYLON

The 630s's abilities and improved ergonomics made it popular on the farm.

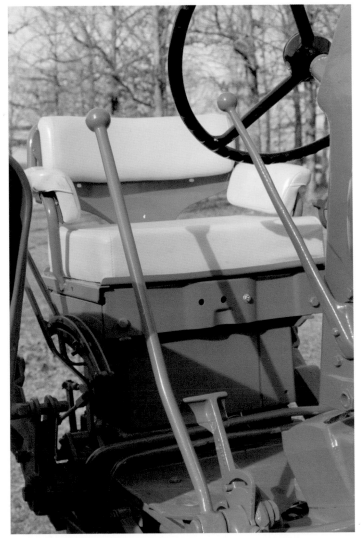

▲ Just over 50 belt hp was available with a belt attached to the spinning clutch of the versatile John Deere 630.

◄ This tractor – like many restored John Deeres – has the optional Float-Ride seat.

Above: A series of bosses were a part of the 630's grille and could be used for hanging implements or counter-weights.

Top Right: Power to drive accessories was supplied via hydraulic outlets found at the rear of the 630.

Right: As we find on many John Deere models, the dual tricycle wheel option was popular.

Far Left: The angular fenders used on most 630s carried a pair of headlights for added after-dark productivity.

Above: When ordered with the LPG option, the fuel tank rode high and towards the rear of the more-contoured hood of the John Deere 630.

Far Left: A nicely-optioned 630 with fenders, headlights and power steering.

Photographed on a rainy day, the valuable 4010 seat was covered for protection.

ntroduced during "Dallas Texas Deere Days" in October 1960, the 4010 was the largest tractor in the company's catalog and one of the New-Generation John Deere tractors. Setting a new standard for motorized farming was a 75-hp engine. Along with enhanced power, the 4010 was loaded with innovations that put it ahead of the competition.

After toying with V-6s, John Deere settled on an in-line six-cylinder engine because it was best in efficiency, power creation and cost of assembly. The 380-cid engine could produce up to 84 hp, depending on the fuel supply used. Deere claimed that the 4010 was up to nearly any chore.

Mounted to the new motor was an eight-speed Synchro-Range gearbox. Its eight forward gears were teamed with three reverse ratios for the ultimate in selection. In top gear, the 4010 could reach a speed of 14.25 mph. That was with a tractor that weighed just under than five tons, when topped off with fuel and fluids.

The 4010 offered three fuel options: gasoline, LPG or diesel. There were four chassis types: standard, row-crop, high-crop and industrial. The front axle could be fitted with a single tire, dual-tricycle tires or the Roll-O-Matic option.

Seen here is a 4010 Diesel with a 34-gallon fuel tank. The seven main bearings in the diesel engine compared to four mains in the gas and LPG engines.

One of the biggest innovations on the 4010 was a central hydraulic system. A variable pump that could flex and meet with changing needs for pressure replaced the older system that discharged excess oil. The variable-pump system controlled the three-point hitch, power steering, power brakes and locking differential.

Combining the talents of Henry Dreyfuss and Associates with orthopedic specialist Dr. Janet Travell, the saddle seat of the John Deere 4010 set new standards for comfort and ergonomics.

This particular 1960 model is a wheatland tractor featuring a standard, fixed-width front axle. Its steel wheels carry 7.50 x 18-L front tires and 18.4 x 34 rear tires. The man who owns this 4010 already owned a John Deere 3020 Standard and knew that a 4010 was just what he needed to fill an empty space in his barn.

When new, the 4010's base price range was $4,116 to $5,286, depending on configuration and wheel selection. Choosing the optional diesel power plant added $700 to the total. A three-point hitch cost $179.

Nearly 58,000 copies of the 4010 were sold during its years of production, 1960-1963. Of those, more than 36,000 were diesel-powered row-crop models. A single gasoline-powered row-crop tractor was also built. Later, this unit was returned to the John Deere factory and retro-fitted with a diesel engine.

1960 4010

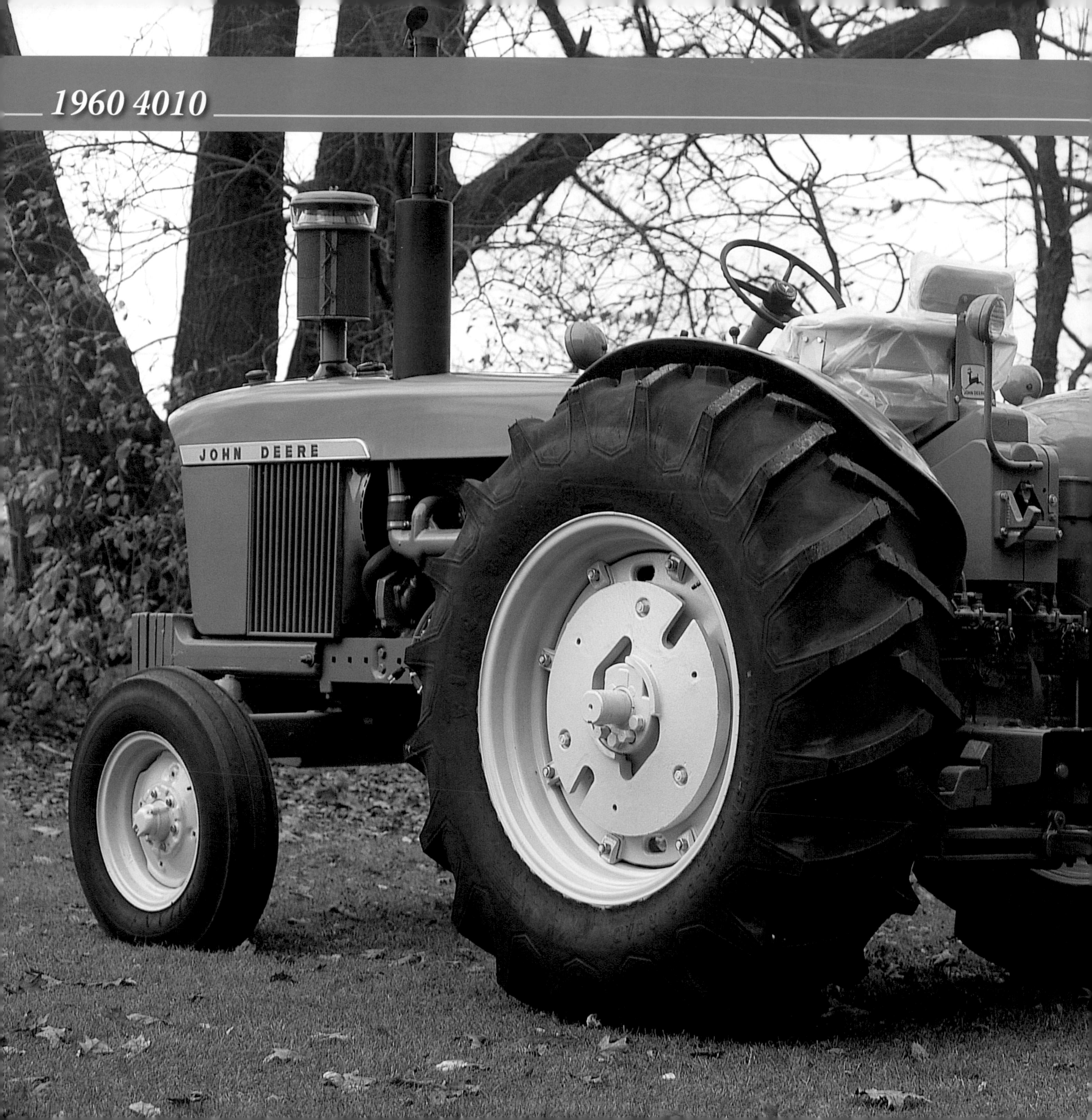

The "business end" of this 1960 John Deere 4010 could handle lots of accessories.

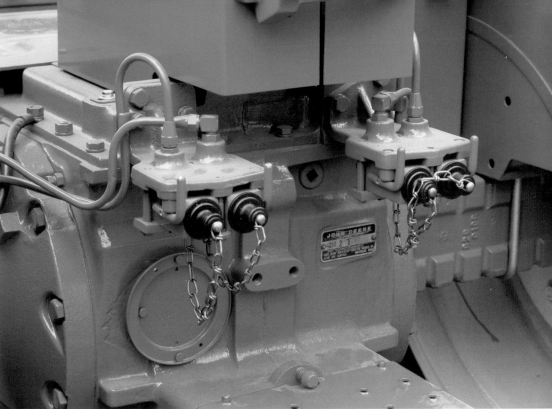

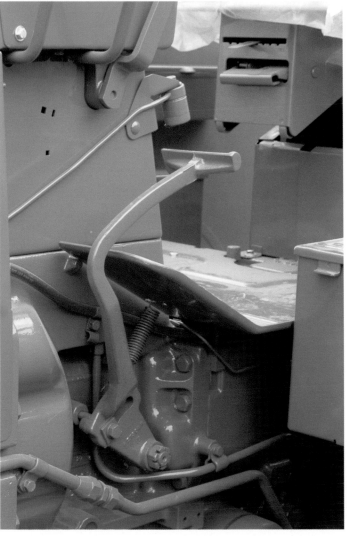

▲ A central hydraulic system with multiple outlets allowed a variety of accessories to be attached and put to use.

◄ The length and shape of the foot-operated pedals was important for proper leverage.

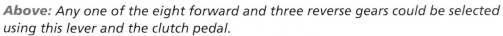

Above: *Any one of the eight forward and three reverse gears could be selected using this lever and the clutch pedal.*

Top Right: *Used to keep the front end down when pulling heavy accessories, these weights can be easily attached to the front of the 4010 chassis.*

Right: *Ribbed tires were mounted on this wheatland model.*

Far Left: Easy-to-read gauges were placed around a large central instrument that showed rpm, gear selections and speed and hours of use.

Left: The 4010's three-point hitch could be fixed in several positions to match the profile of the accessory it had to pull.

ERE

4010 DIESEL

The in-line six-cylinder engine in the 4010 produced up to 84 hp.

1966 3020

This 3020 is a utility model with wide-spaced row-crop front wheel configuration.

n 1964, as part of its never-ending desire to stay ahead of competitiors, John Deere replaced the 3010 with the 3020. Envisioned as a "tractor for all reasons," the 3020 was sold in different engine and chassis configurations. Gas, LPG and diesel engines were on the menu. The standard Synchro-Range eight-speed transmission could be upgraded to a "Power-Shift" version with eight forward gears and two extra reverse gears.

This 3020 was built as a utility tractor with a row-crop front wheel configuration and with row-crop type rear fenders. The front wheels are designed to be adjustable to widths between 59 inches and 79 inches. The rear axle could also be adjusted to work with the front track. This kind of flexibility added to buyer demand for the 3020.

A 270-cid diesel engine rated at 2,500 rpm with 71.26 belt hp was fitted in this tractor. A 29-gallon fuel tank provided plenty of endurance for long days working the fields. A smaller 227-cid engine was used in gas and LPG versions of the 3020, though all three produced about the same power.

To provide extreme versatility, this 3020 has been equipped with front and rear hydraulic outlets for attaching ancillary equipment. The owner of this tractor likes its low seat and easy access. The low height also allows it to fit in buildings with lower doors.

This tractor was actually purchased new with the idea of adding it to a collection in mind. It was therefore ordered with just about every option a single machine could hold, including John Deere's traction-lock system.

Weighing in at just under 10,000 pounds, the 3020 was a mid-range model. It was first sold as a 1964 model and sales continued through 1972. In 1967, prices ranged from $6,525 for the gas-fueled row-crop version to $7,100 for the diesel row-crop version. Changes for 1968 included the availability of John Deere's Front-Wheel-Assist option. In 1969, the gas and LPG versions switched to using a larger-displacement engine, although the diesel engine did not change. In 1969, changes were made to the right side operator's console and the electrical system.

Though purchased with collecting in mind, this John Deere 3020 was used for planting, mowing, baling and cultivating. Its use for such diverse tasks illustrates the versatility of the 3020.

This front "bumper" gives this handsome tractor a hefty front overhang.

JOHN DEERE

3020
DIESEL

▲ A low seat height made this 3020 easy to climb on via the steel steps.

◄ The gauges on the 3020 were compact, but gave complete information.

Above: *Weight could be added up front to balance large accessories pulled behind the tractor.*

Top Right: *Twin air filters contributed to a clean-running engine.*

Right: *Providing the 3020 with clean air to breath was the job of the intake stack.*

Far Left: The 270-cid four-cylinder diesel motor was used in this 3020.

Left: A pair of row-crop fenders was optional on this tractor.

The 3020 was first sold as a 1964 model and sales continued up until 1972.

1966 4020 *High-Crop*

The 4020 was again an improved version of a previous John Deere product.

Companies that manufacture things usually come up with certain milestone products that stand out as class leaders. Ford had the Mustang, Chevrolet had the Corvette and Harley-Davidson had the Knucklehead. In the world of John Deere tractors, the 4020 usually garners more than its fair share of "positive votes" from serious collectors.

This tractor's owner grew interested in a high-crop 4020 owned by a good friend. He was soon searching the collector marketplace for one of these New-Generation models to call his own. Fortunately, a local dealer had a pair of 4020s in stock. The man picked the earlier of the two tractors, which featured the Power-Shift option. He bought it and he took his new prize home to begin a restoration.

As is the case with many new models, the 4020 was actually the improved successor of a previous tractor. It made its bow in 1964. Basically, John Deere blended the high points of the 4010 with some even better features to create this industry-leading product.

Gasoline, diesel and LPG engines were offered for the 4020. In 1964-1965, a 340-cid gas engine was used. The displacement of the gas engine increased to 362 cubic inches in 1966-1972 models. A 404-cid in-line six-cylinder diesel is used in the 4020 pictured here. This engine was rated at 2200 rpm. Also available was a 2,500-rpm version that was equipped with a foot throttle for paved-road operation. The diesel set buyers back an extra $820 in 1965, but the long-term fuel savings could quickly offset the higher price.

Early models of the 4020 were available with a new Power-Shift transmission that required just one hand to operate. Eight forward and four reverse gears were on tap, providing plenty of flexibility for any task. With no clutch engagement required, the $630 Power-Shift option brought a new level of convenience to farmers. The only minor downside to Power-Shift was the loss of a small amount of horsepower.

A standard Synchro-Range manual gearbox was more common on these tractors, but was not as easy to operate as the Power-Shift transmission. However, the Power-Shift option sold for $630 in 1965, a price high enough to keep some buyers away. Operating within the 1,500- to 2,200-rpm range, the 4020 could move from 1.23 mph to 18.7 mph forward and from 1.44 mph to 5.17 mph in reverse.

Like other John Deere models, the 4020 was sold in standard, row-crop and high-crop models, each coming with the different engine possibilities. The sales leader with production of 36,736 units was the row-crop model with diesel power. Its production was over three times the number standard models (11,370) built with diesel engines. With a 34-gallon fuel tank, the 4020 ran a long time between fill-ups.

Additional features of this 4020 include dual hydraulics and front and rear PTOs.

▲ The front axle of this 4020 high-crop tractor provides clearance for working taller crops.

◀ The front cowl of the John Deere 4020 is a strong styling element.

Above: *On the rear of this John Deere are 18.4 x 34-inch rice-and-cane tires.*

Top Right: *The 404-cid in-line six-cylinder diesel engine produces 94 hp.*

Right: *The rear axle provides added clearance on the High-Crop 4020.*

Additional features on this 1966 John Deere 4020 include dual hydraulics and front and rear independent PTOs that offer 540-rpm or 1,000-rpm operational speeds. Headlights and a cigarette lighter in the dash are added convenience items. Being a high-crop model, the tractor has a full 32 inches of clearance below it. Its rear tire spacing can be adjusted to varying widths between 73 and 97 inches, according to the type of work the farmer has in mind. The reversible, deep-well rims are mounted to cast-iron wheels. This 4020 wears 7.50 x 20 tri-rib front tires and 18.4 x 34 rice-and-cane rear tires.

The front-three-quarter view gives the green machine a "praying mantis" look.

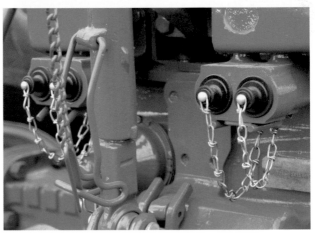

Above: The universal, three-point hitch can pull any accessory behind the John Deere 4020.

Top Right: There are plenty of ports where hydraulic accessories can be attached on this tractor.

High-horsepower tractors were more in evidence as the 1960s unfolded. The 5020 was one of many models in John Deere's New-Generation line and it was a large tractor with a big diesel engine. In Standard configuration, it had a shipping weight of 13,560 pounds and a test weight of more than 21,000 pounds. A puny power plant was not going to move a 5020 around very well.

To handle the job of moving efficiently, Deere equipped this tractor with a 531.6-cid six-cylinder diesel motor of John Deere manufacture. The valve-in-head engine used a 16.5:1 compression ratio. Power on the 1966 model was rated at a maximum of 133.25 PTO hp. Later, in 1969, the horsepower number would go up to 141.34 PTO hp.

Originally responsible for bringing the 5020's big diesel to life was a 24-volt electrical system that utilized four, 6-volt batteries. However, John Deere 5020s with serial numbers higher than 25000 carried a 12-volt system.

Deere's Synchro-Range transmission was used in the 5020. It provided eight forward gears and three reverse ratios that allowed the versatile tractor to handle a dizzying variety of tasks. Provisions for the attachment of many accessories also added to the tractor's usefulness.

Keeping the big diesel fed was a 68-gallon fuel tank. Although the 5020 was a sizeable machine, it still returned decent fuel mileage and this allowed for extended working days on a farm. In Nebraska Tractor Test No. 947, a 1966 Model 5020, operating in fourth gear, made the two-hour economy run at 113.72 maximum drawbar hp. This yielded economy of 13.85 hp-hours per gallon of fuel and a pull of 8,529 pounds at 5.41 mph with 3.76-percent slippage.

Standard equipment on the 5020 included dual 18.4-38 rear wheels and 9.50-20-inch front tires. When it was fitted with a hydraulic hitch, the 5020 operated smoothly in raising or lowering various farming equipment. Protective steel panels kept stray debris from reaching the operator and helped to add to the svelte lines of the big 5020.

To keep the manufacturing process simple and cost efficient, John Deere offered the 5020 only in standard and row-crop configurations. The retail price tag for the standard version was $14,600.

Left: Although a sizeable unit, the 5020 managed to deliver decent fuel mileage.

1966 5020 *Standard*

Protective steel panels kept stray debris from reaching the operator of the big 5020.

▲ The easy-to-read gauge array avoided unnecessary bells and whistles.

◀ Climbing on the 5020 was accomplished using the steel steps on the sides of the chassis.

Above: *Adding counterweights up front gave better balance for pulling heavy implements.*

Top Right: *The 5020's front axle was width-adjustable so different crops could be cultivated.*

Right: *The 3-point hydraulic hitch could deliver smooth operation of accessories.*

Far Left: The 5020's in-line, six-cylinder diesel provided ample power for most fieldwork.

Left: Steering the 5020 was a matter of twisting this black-rimmed steering wheel.

The exhaust manifold on the 5020's diesel engine was another massive casting.

1966 5020 *Dual*

Call-outs decorating the cowl
announce the big 531-cid diesel
power plant.

For the most part, the history of John Deere is a rolling out of bigger and better tractors, each based on a previous model. As a youth, Randy Schweer had watched the massive John Deere Model 830 in action. He had been awed by the sheer size of this huge farming machine. Years later, it was the Model 5010 — the most powerful Deere to roam the fields — that caught his attention. Next came Deere's 5020, a follow-up to the big 5010. By then, Randy knew the time had come. When a 5020 became available, he did not waste a moment before deciding to bring it home. The unit required a full restoration, but he knew that nothing could please him more than owning it.

By 1960, the big 830 had proven its worth, but its 75-hp rating fell short of modern-day needs. In 1962, the 5010 stepped up to the plate, with a nearly 120-hp rating, and took the crown. It would be built through 1965. By then, the farming industry was lusting for even more power.

The year 1966 saw the introduction of the new 5020, which carried a 531-cid six-cylinder diesel engine with 10 percent more horsepower than the 5010's engine. This four-cycle power plant featured an overhead valve configuration. With a 16.5:1 compression ratio, it cranked out a 2,200-rpm rating.

Starting the massive diesel engine required a 24-volt electrical system with four six-volt batteries. A separate 12-volt system was used to illuminate the lights and accessories.

Behind the engine was a John Deere Synchro-Range eight-speed gearbox. This transmission actually provided four primary gear ratios, each having a high and low range on tap. Three reverse gears were provided with the lowest ratios. Needless to say, the big 5020 was a breeze to handle during complicated farming maneuvers. The speed range varied from 1.5 mph to more than 20 mph when the foot-throttle-governor override was engaged.

Only a standard version of this tractor was offered in 1966. This '66 model features an optional dual-rear-wheel arrangement. A row-crop model arrived in 1967, the second year of production.

Weighing 17,900 pounds, the 5020 was no lightweight tractor. It could carry 68 gallons of diesel fuel in its tank. This allowed for fairly long runs between refills. Special features on this particular tractor include wide rear fenders and operator dust shields that protect the farmer from debris. The wide-swing drawbar is capable of handling heavier loads than a standard one can. A pair of hydraulic outlets on this tractor provides a power point for various accessories.

The front axle on Randy's 5020 is of the fixed-width style, but it can be set at either 69 or 71 inches. A set of 11.00 x 16 BF Goodrich 8-ply tri-rib front tires handles the steering chores. The rack-and-pinion rear axle can be adjusted to varying tread widths. The dual-drive tires are enormous 18.4 x 34 eight-ply models mounted on 34-inch cast-iron rims. This provides a full 16 inches of ground clearance and allows the monstrous 5020 to skirt the tops of even the deepest furrows.

The running-deer logo decorates the seat pedestal between the dual rear tires.

▲ Dual hydraulic outlets deliver ample power and flexibility for attaching tools.

◀ The 8-ply tri-rib front tires are mounted to reversible 7.50-inch wide rims.

Above: The front cowl of the 5020 has plenty of cooling slats and carries the company name.

Top Right: Simple gauges keep the farmer informed as to the status of the 5020's operation.

Right: This lever and a set of 12-inch clutch plates activate the multi-speed gearbox.

Far Left: This massive cast-iron manifold proves that there is nothing dainty about the 5020.

Left: The heavy-duty 5020's wide-swing drawbar can handle the most severe loads.

This super-traction machine could also do a good job lighting the fields after dark.

An amber lamp let motorists know when a slow-moving tractor was on the road ahead.

Building on the success of the early 2510, the John Deere 2520 upped the ante for 1969. Though the 2510 was a classic design, there had been a few trifling complaints about it at first. These problems were corrected during its production run and provided the 2520 with a "clean slate" to be built upon. The 2520 was a lower-cost alternative to the 4020. However, despite its lower price, it still provided buyers with a "toolbox" full of features that permitted all manners of use on the farm.

Like many models that left the John Deere Works in Waterloo, Iowa, in 1969, the 2520 model got to use a more powerful motor the company had developed. The gasoline-fueled version of the 2520 used a 202.7-cid four-cylinder Deere-built engine that developed 56.98 PTO horsepower. In diesel tractors, the power plant used was a 219.8-cid four-cylinder that generated 61.29 maximum PTO horsepower.

The 2520 seen here is a diesel model that has also been outfitted with the Power-Shift transmission. According to the owner, it is one of only 817 such tractors that were configured this way. The selective-gear fixed-ratio Power-Shift gearbox provides the operator with eight forward speeds and four reverse gears. The tractor has a top speed of just over 17 mph, which makes it slightly faster than the Synchro-Range equipped version. The list price of the 1969 Model 2520 was $5,166. The diesel option added $650 to that and the Power-Shift transmission was a $780 add on.

Just like modern cars have more amenities than '70s cars, most tractors of that era lacked the safety and convenience features we see today. However, the 2520 was a bit ahead of the curve. It offered John Deere's Roll-Over Protection System, also known as ROPS. This 1969 edition has both the ROPS option and a protective canopy top. An even sturdier Roll-Gard cab option was also available for the 2520, if further protection was deemed necessary. However, high-crop versions of the 2520 could not be optioned with the canopy or Roll-Gard cab due to their extraordinary overall height.

The weight of the diesel-powered Power-Shift 2520 was 9,040 pounds when tested. Other versions weighed slightly less, but were still heavy tractors. Part of the explanation for this is that the 2520 came with a very impressive assortment of standard equipment. Power steering, power brakes, a deluxe seat and a fuel gauge were all a part of the tractor's standard package.

Naturally, a lengthy list of optional equipment was also available. In addition to the extras already mentioned, buyers could order two- or three-way hydraulics, the adjustable-width front axle and a three-point "fast" hitch. Such items added immensely to the versatility of this tractor.

The John Deere 2520 tractor's front-end options include this adjustable-width axle.

Top Left: *A full compliment of instruments kept the farmer abreast of functional operation.*

Top: *Eight speeds were included in the 2520's gearbox.*

Left: *The 2520 diesel produced ample power to serve the farmer well in all his chores*

Above: The 2520's steel cowl had mounting points to accept useful accessories.

Top Right: With a series of pre-selected front-axle settings, a variety of harvesting requirements could be met with a 2520.

Right: Three variations of front wheels and tires were available for the 2520.

Far Left: A front axle that adjusted for different types of planting was an option for 2520s.

Left: This three-point hitch on the 2520 could accept whatever equipment the operator needed for a job.

This 2520 has ROPS and a canopy to keep the farmer safe and comfortable at work.

1972 6030 Dual

The factory-optional fenders on this John Deere 6030 give a good measure of protection to the operator.

The powerful 5020 featured in the previous section of this book served John Deere customers well, but eventually tractor buyers started clamoring for even more power. The ever-increasing size and complexity of useful attachments required a tractor that could pull and power them and the 6030 was born out of this need. Using the successful formula of the 5020 and enhancing the output virtually guaranteed that this awesome new agricultural monster would be successful.

The new 6030 could be purchased with a choice of two engines. The standard engine was a 531-cid six-cylinder turbocharged and inter-cooled diesel. This version was rated at 2,100 rpm with 175.99 PTO horsepower on tap. Because some farmers felt that they did not need an engine as powerful as this, in 1973 a 141-hp naturally-aspirated engine was also made available.

A majority of the Gen II 6030s were delivered with an enclosed cab that extended a farmer's comfort and safety. However, the tractor reviewed here was ordered without the cab and is referred to as the "open station" version. Although lacking the cab, this unit does utilize side panels to protect its operator from random debris that might hit him while farming. The oversized 18.4 x 16L tires mounted on the front of this unit are capable of throwing large clods of dirt the operator's way. The factory rubber was 9.50 x 20 in size and cut a narrower swath through the fields. To suit different types of farming, the front axle is adjustable to a number of different widths.

This 6030 features a John Deere Synchro-Range eight-speed gearbox with two reverse ratios. The huge tractor takes 73 gallons of diesel fuel in a single fill-up and requires 40 quarts of coolant to keep the temperatures in line. Even the hydraulic system requires 16 gallons of hydraulic fluid to operate accessories like a three-point hitch that is capable of hoisting more than 5,900 pounds. A 1,000-rpm PTO is also included to power any motorized accoutrements that the farmer wants to run off the rear outlets.

The giant John Deere 6030 had a 104-inch wheelbase and came standard with a single set of rear tires. However, this tractor carries a pair of 20.8 x 38 dual rear tires for added traction. Weighing in at nearly 8 tons, the 6030 is no featherweight. It's a hardworking rig that can be used to accomplish a wide variety of duties around a farm.

The acquisition of this standard 6030 took some time because the original owner was hesitant to sell it. Because of its odd, open-station configuration, the current owner was keen on adding it to his collection and kept up negotiations for two years. The prize was well worth the wait, however. As it turned out, when the original owner's son finally agreed to sell the tractor, the deal included an eight-bottom plow that had been purchased along with the tractor when it was new. The buyer also received a lot of documentation and service books as part of the deal.

The 6030 would be built until 1977. Then, an even more powerful model supplanted it.

An owner's name tag on right frame rail identifies this as a collector's item.

JOHN DEER

1972 6030
Randy & Sharon Sterwa

▲ Counterweights enable the tractor to lift nearly three tons with a rear-mounted hydraulic hitch.

◄ These wider-than-standard 18.4 x 16L tires help to reduce compaction in the field.

Right: *Lights were provided on the rear of this tractor for field lighting and road-use safety.*

Below: *This open station model lacks an enclosed cabin, but does have protective shields.*

Lower Right: *The in-line six-cylinder diesel engine produced 176 hp with a turbocharger or 141 hp without it.*

Far Left: The width of the 6030's front axle can be adjusted to match the crops being cultivated.

Above: Fully adjustable for speed, the hydraulic outlets on the 6030 are as sensitive as they are strong.

Left: The optional steel fenders cover the inside set of tires, but not the outside ones.

With all those tires churning, it's a good thing the operator rides inside the cabin.

The size and sophistication of mid-1970s farming operations resulted in John Deere and other tractor manufacturers having to build bigger and more powerful machines to keep pace with demand. As the average acreage of the typical farm grew larger, so did the size of the machinery needed to work the land. Eventually, a large four-wheel-drive tractor seemed to be the sensible choice for many farms.

Adding drive to a tractor's second axle to provide four-wheel drive requires more than just a stronger running gear. Power and power-transmission issues must also be addressed. These are considerations that had been with John Deere designers since they created the company's first four-wheel-drive model in 1961.

That first Deere model to feature drive wheels at all four corners was called to 8010.Its success early in the game led to development of the 8020 in 1964. After that, the use of this new rage in tractor design continued to expand. John Deere's line of four-wheel-drive models kept growing. A real highlight was the release of the 7020, which debuted in 1971. This tractor combined the strongest points of earlier models with new levels of comfort and convenience for the operator.

Steering a tractor as large as a 7020 required that the chassis be able to bend around tight turns, so an articulated design was decided upon. Perhaps, the only thing more difficult than turning a non-articulated 10-ton tractor is designing a "hinged" frame.

Luckily, John Deere's Research and Development department got the job done.

The giant 7020 was powered by a 146-hp turbocharged and inter-cooled diesel engine designed to produce maximum power. To match the output of the engine, an eight-speed Synchro-Range transmission, fitted with Deere's Hi-Lo option, could be ordered. This option doubled the number of gear ratios at hand so that speeds up to 21.6 mph could be attained.

When Deere launched the 7520 — a tractor based on the 7020 — it increased power to 175 hp. The installation of a fully-enclosed Roll-Gard cockpit also brought a new level of comfort to the equation. This cockpit or cabin served to keep dirt and debris from hitting the driver, but also facilitated heating and air conditioning the operator's working environment. Power steering and power brakes made the 7520 safer to drive and gave it better handling.

For rigorous work, the 7520 included a third remote-cylinder hydraulic outlet. It could be teamed with a three-point hitch with a Quik-Coupler to ease the installation and removal of accessories. Adding to the usefulness of the 7520 was a rear-driven 1,000-rpm PTO. To make sure the farmer's day in the fields wouldn't get cut short, the 7520 carried 156 gallons of diesel in two separate tanks. One of the tanks was mounted on each side of the chassis, but both were filled from a common port. Considering the relatively

1974 7520

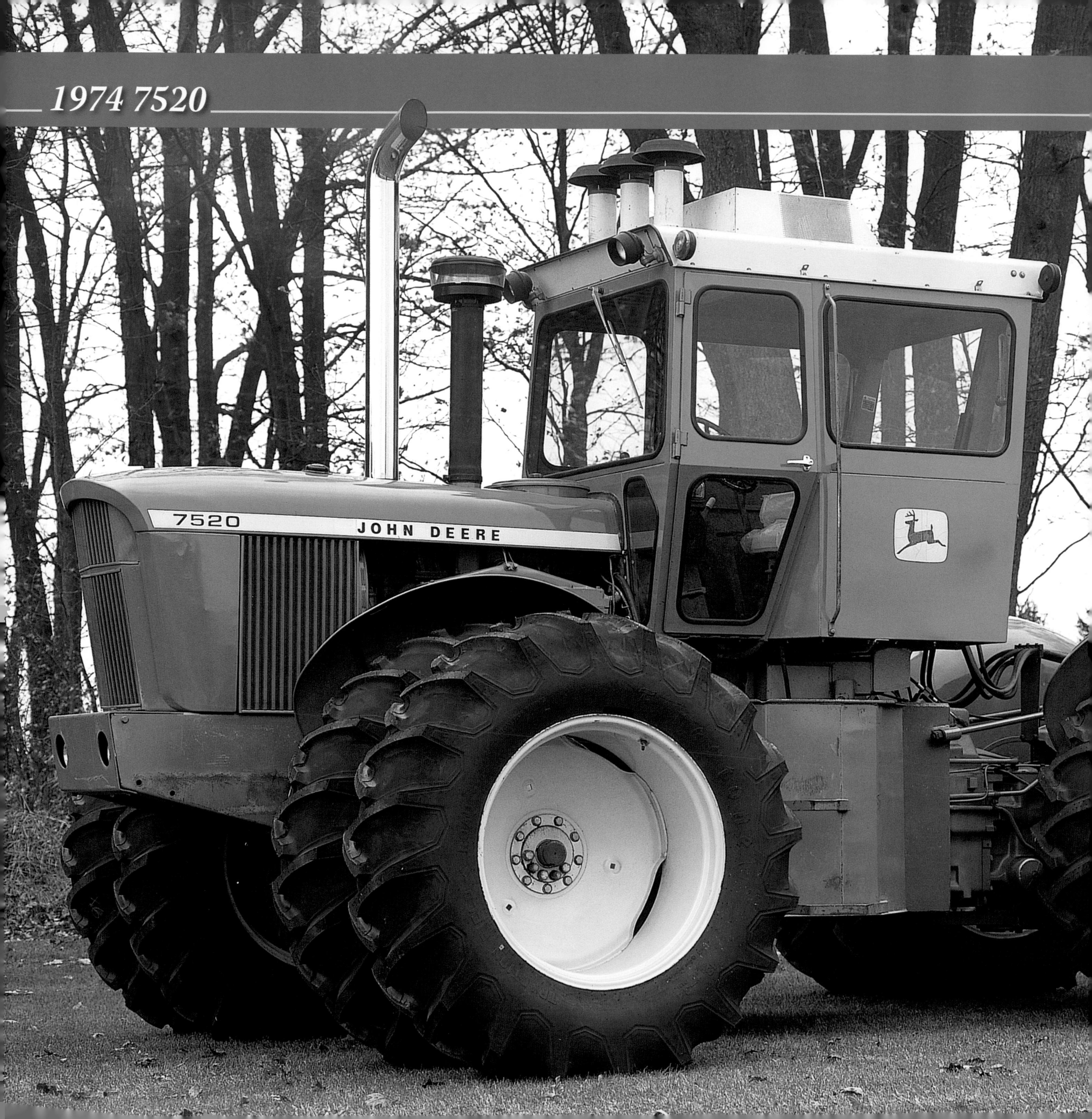

The John Deere 7520 tips the scales at a very-nicely distributed 20,000 pounds.

▲ Two tanks carry 156 gallons of diesel fuel and provide access steps to the cabin.

◄ Every function of the 7520 is aided by the tractor's many heavy-duty features.

Top Right: *It's tough to miss a 7520 when its equipped with dual tires at all four corners.*

Middle Right: *A trio of breather stacks on the cabin provide comfortable filtered ventilation.*

Lower Right: *The three-point hitch has a Quik-Coupler option for speedy implement hook ups.*

Below: *A fully enclosed, air-conditioned Roll-Gard cabin makes for comfortable farming.*

high mileage rating of the big 7520, the fuel supply could last a long, long time.

To provide outstanding traction and handling, the featured 7520 model was fitted with a set of eight 18.4 x 34 rear tires. The large tires improve its weight-distribution characteristics and also reduce soil compaction.

The owner of this 7520 actually had another one in his collection earlier. He gave it up and, then, regretted that he had sold it. He found this replacement in Colorado and wasted no time purchasing it. Within a week, he had another 7520 under his roof.

◀ The 175-hp turbocharged and inter-cooled 7520 beats efficiency of many big tractors.

First in a line of Ertl's Precision models, this John Deere GP with cultivators was released in 1992 and is appropriately marked "Number 1."

As much as many of us would like to have a barn loaded with full-size John Deere tractors, dealing with the storage of such a collection is not a possibility for most of us.

For those still desiring to collect John Deere tractors, there is a more convenient way to satisfy that lust – scale models. Miniature versions of many John Deere tractors can be purchased from stores, catalogs and Websites.

A dizzying variety of John Deere models, toys and collectibles can be found and all of them can be purchased for a fraction of what the "Real McCoy" might set you back. In addition, you can display your collection of models in a much smaller space than that required to store real tractors. In some cases, model tractors can be displayed in a manner that allows viewing them all at a single glance.

Of the many makers of miniature farm machines available today, the Ertl Company of Dyersville, Iowa, has become the leader. This manufacturer is constantly bringing new and more-highly-detailed die-cast collectibles to the market. From the most basic replicas to precision models, Ertl produces little tractors and agricultural apparatus at prices to fit almost any budget. Many of the company's products are scaled-down versions of the equipment made by another Iowa company – John Deere.

With a history that stretches back to 1945, early examples of Ertl products are scarce and bring premium prices. As kids, few of us had the foresight to protect and cherish such miniatures. If only we had known how much they'd be worth some day!

The unstyled Model L was one of John Deere's smaller early tractors. It was captured in full detail, by SpecCast, in this 1/16-scale version.

Regardless, you can still find and buy many of the John Deere tractors and implements that Ertl has made copies of. You can start your collection right now by making purchases at charity stores, garage sales, second-hand shops, hobby outlets, flea markets and auctions, as well as through collector magazines and Websites.

All the John Deere collectibles pictured on these pages were created in 1/16-scale, which lends itself well to a high degree of detail, as well as a convenient in size for in-home storage. Ertl is only one of several companies offering such items, but Ertl is the favorite of a John Deere collector we met while doing this book. He has only that brand (and color scheme) in his trophy room, thus limiting our coverage to Ertl models. As you can see, that gave us plenty of miniatures to shoot pictures of.

An unstyled BW was the focus of this die-cast replica. Ertl chose both solid and spoke wheels for this miniature.

This scaled-down John Deere Model A carries a replica John Deere umbrella.

Carrying the John Deere name on a protective umbrella, this GP replica is shown out of its Ertl factory packaging.

This John Deere Model A is finished in gleaming gold and labeled as the "Toy of the Century."

A measure of the detail that Ertl strives for in their models is exemplified by the scale tire chains that encompass the drive tires of this miniature John Deere 720.

This John Deere 720 is equipped with both a front loader and a rear blade. A weatherbreak wraps the cockpit. In real life, this device retained heat from the tractor to keep the operator warm.

🦌 Ertl and SpecCast

Looking at the detail of the 1/16-scale John Deere Model D, you can almost imagine the big motor chugging away as its flywheel spins.

Showing the range of models Ertl sells, here we see a 1/16- and 1/64-scale examples of the John Deere Model D. Both were released in 1994.

An earlier miniature version of the John Deere Model D is featured in this Ertl collectible, which includes steel "skeleton" wheels.

The "Waterloo Boy" is another famous tractor that Ertl captured in full detail. This is another of the toy company's many precision models and a real favorite with collectors.

Many of the SpecCast models come with implements, as we see on this John Deere Model M with a two-bottom moldboard plow.

Ertl and SpecCast

Ertl made this pint-size John Deere
Model H with dual-tricycle front wheels.

One of the prettiest John Deere products was the Orchard tractor. This 1993 Ertl model was a special edition of the John Deere 620 Orchard Tractor.

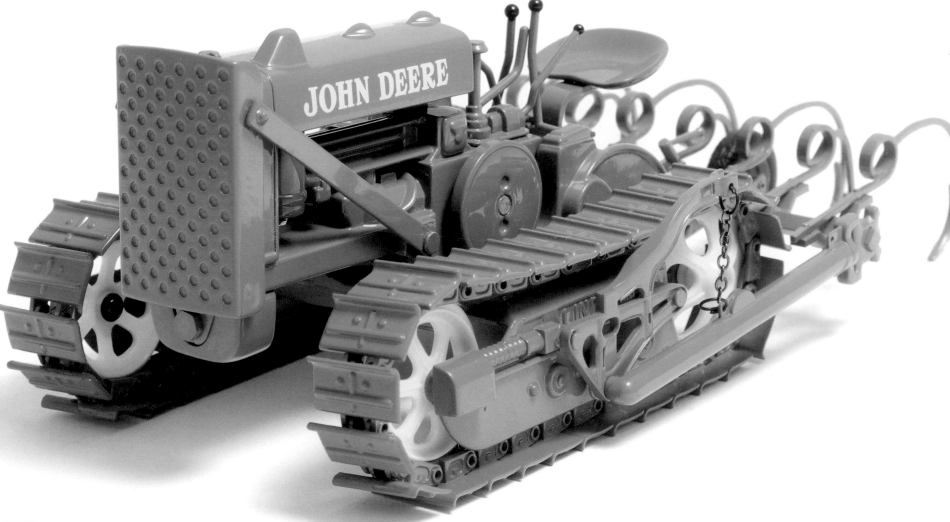

Lindeman converted John Deere tractors into crawlers and this scale model of one by SpecCast features a rear-mounted cultivator.

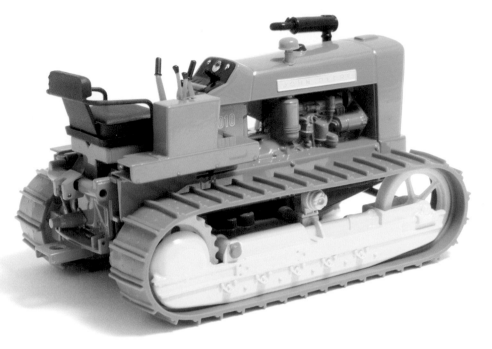

Later versions of the Lindeman crawler were made by John Deere. This is an Ertl replica of the John Deere 1010 model.

A tiny farmer gets ready to inspect his John Deere 45 combine, a scale model of the first self-propelled unit in that market.

This 1/16th-scale Ertl model shows a Model 60 equipped with a corn picker-sheller. The matching scale trailer is being filled with replica corn.

Whether it's connected to a scale hay baler or rolling across the fields by itself, this Ertl Model B looks terrific in any collection.